Early Praise for Building Profit through Building People

The 5-star management model that Carrig and Wright present is more than just another theory of business. Using actual data from SYSCO Corporation, they demonstrate convincingly that the effective management of people is a key driver of business success—with payoffs to employees, customers, and shareholders. They lay out a blueprint that both managers and scholars will find richly rewarding.

—Wayne F. Cascio, Ph.D., *US Bank Term Professor of Management, The Business School, University of Colorado-Denver and Health Sciences Center*

Every page of this pithy volume crackles with insights and guidelines for managing people in ways that drive better business results while enhancing the quality of working life. And it is real life stuff—every key point is supported with right-on examples and/or rock solid data. The authors' value-profit chain will dominate strategic thinking in customer-driven businesses for a long time to come.

—Lee Dyer, *Professor—Human Resource Studies, Cornell University*

Finally business is getting it…when you build your people, you build your business. HR has for years been thought of as a soft support function. Ken Carrig and Pat Wright reveal, step by step, a process to make it a powerful force for business growth.

—Rick Goings, *Chairman & Chief Executive Officer, Tupperware Corporation*

Carrig and Wright provide evidence that theory works. This book takes us step-by-step through the important and complex process of linking people to profit. If linking people to profit is your challenge, this is a book for you. Carrig and Wright speak with authority borne out of first-hand, practical knowledge.

—James Heskett, *co-author of* The Value Profit Chain

It starts with carefully selected symbols, right key messages, and committed leaders who motivate their followers. Then add simple processes to build or sustain momentum and use key metrics to steer by. These are building blocks to 5-STAR organization excellence. Ken Carrig and Pat Wright both tell a story and demonstrate how others can create their own story for success. The path is clear, the journey is up to the reader. There are lessons here for beginners, established professionals, and masters of the art of managing and leading people in organizations.

—John Hofmeister, *President, Shell Oil Company*

It is not common to find a book so well structured around real life examples and practical-proven tools to help companies and organizations to unleash the full potential of their people. The authors demonstrate how the Value-Profit Chain model can make a difference not just for employee commitment but bottom-line financial success.

—J. Randall MacDonald, *Senior Vice President Human Resources—* *IBM Corporation*

Carrig and Wright bring together a unique combination of skills with academic rigor coupled with real world instinct. The Continental and SYSCO stories offer HR professionals everywhere with ideas and tools that can be adapted and applied. Their work shows specifically how to do strategic HR work and when strategic HR happens, companies succeed. The book is easy to use, well written, and pragmatic. It shows what can happen when good ideas are implemented by good people.

—Dave Ulrich, *Professor, Ross School of Business, Author,* HR Value Proposition *and* Why The Bottom Line Isn't

Building
PROFIT
through Building
PEOPLE

Building
PROFIT
through Building
PEOPLE

Making Your Workforce
the Strongest Link
in the Value-Profit Chain

Ken Carrig and
Patrick M. Wright

Society for Human Resource Management
Alexandria, Virginia
USA
www.shrm.org

The Society for Human Resource Management (SHRM) is the world's largest association devoted to human resource management. Representing more than 190,000 individual members, the Society serves the needs of HR professionals by providing the most essential and comprehensive set of resources available. As an influential voice, SHRM is committed to advancing the human resource profession to ensure that HR is an essential and effective partner in developing and executing organizational strategy. Visit SHRMOnline at www.shrm.org.

Library of Congress Cataloguing-in-Publication Data
Carrig, Ken, 1957–
    Building profit through building people: how to make people the strongest link in the value-profit chain / Ken Carrig and Patrick M. Wright.
        p. cm.
    ISBN 1-58644-069-1
    1. Employee motivation. 2. Job satisfaction. 3. Employee loyalty. 4. Consumer satisfaction.
5. Corporate profits. 6. Supervision of employees. 7. Personnel management. I. Wright, Patrick M.
II. Society for Human Resource Management (U.S.) III. Title.

HF5549.5.M63C377 2005
658.3'14—dc22

                                                        2005027116

Dedications

The royalties for this book will go to "Share our Strength," an organization dedicated to fighting hunger. We would like to thank them for the good they do for so many and their commitment to not quitting until the fight against hunger is won. For more information, please access the organization's Web site (www.strength.org).

This book is dedicated to my incredible wife, Lisa, my three wonderful children Patrick, Kaitlin, and Emily, and my supportive parents. I also want to acknowledge the SYSCO leadership team and all 50,000 associates at SYSCO who strive to excel each day for our customers.

Ken Carrig

This book is dedicated to the love of my life, my wife Mary, my two wonderful sons, Michael and Matthew, and to my parents, Paul and Patricia Wright, all of whom provided the love and support I needed in completing this project.

Patrick M. Wright

Contents

Figures and Tables

Acknowledgements

As is true for any effort such as this book, far more people contributed than will receive the recognition of authorship. This book could never have been completed had only the two authors been involved, so we want to take this opportunity to express our appreciation for the contributions of those who make it possible.

First, Susan Billiot has been an integral part of the entire process. Working closely with Ken at SYSCO, Susan contributed to the content of the book during its conception and then provided valuable editorial input to the first draft.

Second, Ken Newsome, Ellen Jones, and Denise Smith along with SYSCO's corporate and operating-company HR professionals also contributed tremendously to the content through their work in developing the "How to Become a 5-STAR Company" booklet. This booklet was a valuable resource for us to communicate externally the ideas that it communicates internally within the SYSCO family of companies.

Third, Amy C. Baker contributed both the insight gained from her eleven-year career in human resources at Dell and her exquisite communication skills to produce a readable book. She took what were often disjointed and disconnected ideas and weaved them into a coherent and, we hope, interesting story.

Fourth, Jo Hagin provided invaluable technical help and support with the early drafts of this book. She managed the Ithaca end of communications going back and forth with Houston and helped to construct a draft copy that our reviewers were able to read easily.

Phyllis Brown's help throughout this project cannot be measured. She managed the Houston end of the project, and produced the cleaned up documents that constituted each draft. Then, when the project reached its final stages, she was the key contributor to constructing the final document, inserting figures and tables in all the right places, and gathering all the appendices and tools available on the SHRM Web site. Her contributions were priceless, and we cannot express enough appreciation for them.

There are others whose ideas and suggestions contributed to this book. Marty Walsh, former Executive Director of the Society for Human Resource Management Foundation consistently championed this book—both to us and to the larger SHRM community. Steve Miranda, SPHR, GPHR, who is now at SHRM, and Manesh K. Rath, Esq. of Keller and Heckman LLP reviewed the text. Ed Gubman from Strategic Talent Solutions reviewed an early draft; his suggestions, and more importantly his encouragement, gave us the initial impetus to get going. Scott Snell at Cornell University always provided a sounding board and valuable feedback on our ideas as the book was in process. Jim Heskett of Harvard University met with us early on and also contributed both advice and encouragement. SYSCO's CEO Rick Schnieders and SYSCO's executive team served as examples of 5-STAR leadership, and we have appreciated their support throughout the process. Ned Walker and Larry Kellner have been kind enough to allow us to use anecdotes from Continental Airlines, and they both model effective leadership approaches as outlined in this book. We have been honored to be associated with thought- and practice-leading HR executives such as Dave Loeser from Celanese, Randy MacDonald from IBM, John Hofmeister from Shell, Mike D'Ambrose, Kevin Barr from Terex, Bill Conaty from GE, Ursula Fairbairn, Bill Maki from Weyerhauser, and John Murabito from Cigna, all of whom have served as role models for the HR profession and whose organizations' stories have supplied the building blocks for the ideas presented here.

Introduction

What would it be like to work at a company whose CEO lived, breathed, and managed with this philosophy?

We have five major constituents: associates, customers, suppliers, communities, and shareholders. If we do our best to be fair to them, we'll not only achieve business success, but live our lives more happily.
   —**John Baugh,** founder and retired chairman of the board, SYSCO Corporation

SYSCO leadership consistently practiced this mantra to drive organizational success. The performance as a result of this approach not only went on to create significant shareholder value but also in the process helped many live their lives more happily. It was the same mantra that turned around Continental Airlines—and that created success at the many other companies described here. To attain greater satisfaction at work, you must not only believe in this principle but also know how to put it into practice. We wrote this book to help leaders in all types of companies implement the mantra that led to measurable success in these two very different companies.

We are most intimately knowledgeable about how SYSCO and Continental implemented these principles, and the working documents and exhibits in the book are from SYSCO. But to show the broad spectrum of success, we have described their use in many different companies, among them Starbucks; Sears; Nordstrom; Southwest Airlines; SAS Institute; Microsoft; and Seibel Systems.

People buy a book like this for different reasons. Some because their company is in trouble, and they need ideas to steer it back in the right direction. Some because their company is doing well, but they know it can do better. Some because they are thinking of starting a new company, and they want to set the right course from the beginning.

Whatever the reason, we think readers will find useful and practical ideas in this field book. Why? Because it is based on the experiences and best practices of different companies: large and small, thriving and barely surviving, global and strictly local.

We believe you will find nuggets of truth here—wherever your business falls on the scale of profitability and employee engagement, however clear your team is on what really makes for success in this competitive environment that we all work in. The principles we set forth are based on real-life and practical experience. We intend for this book to read like a conversation over a cup of coffee with one of your most trusted and wise business associates.

Our goal is to offer tried-and-true tools that will improve your organization's corporate focus on the vital links between employee, customer, and shareholder satisfaction. We will not only review the theory of the value-profit chain (VPC), but also provide specific approaches for evaluating a company's progress along the goals set at critical links in that chain.

In the first two chapters, we describe the VPC and its crucial importance to a company. By focusing specifically on the VPC business philosophy, we will enhance its definition, highlighting the importance of executional excellence and innovative approaches to sustaining profitable growth.

In Chapter 3, we offer ideas on building loyalty among the customers you want to keep. In Chapter 4, we acquaint you with some tried-and-true tools for building the loyalty of your associates and transforming your company into a bona fide employer of choice.

In Chapter 5, you will find examples of tools for sharing best practices and knowledge within your company—a powerful technique for reliable, easily implemented improvements. We also demonstrate, through concrete examples, the importance of thoroughly understanding your business and your people while you transform your business.

In Chapters 6, 7, and 8, we dive deep into the mechanics and practices of establishing your organization as a "5-STAR" employer.

In Chapter 9 are a set of tools and metrics to transform your company into an employer of choice, through user friendly ways of sharing and leveraging knowledge and practices within your company.

In the final chapter, we try to pique your interest in what the future may hold for the human resources function and its role in creating competitive advantage and sustained profitable growth in organizations.

Finally, we offer online versions of some proven templates, forms, and instruments on a section of the Society for Human Resource Management (SHRM) Web site. You can find these at www.shrm.org/books/buildingprofit/tools.

This is not a pie-in-the-sky book that will inspire you briefly and then fade from memory shortly after you finish it. It is a book that you will keep on your desk or in your briefcase. You will dog-ear the pages and scribble notes in the margins. You will find yourself using it, improving on it, and sending relevant sections to your co-workers. You'll even buy extra copies to give to friends—we hope! Our point is that this is a working document, a reference manual, a field book. The more visible you keep it, the more good it will do you and your company.

CHAPTER 1

A Compelling Argument: It's All about People

ertainly today's fast-paced competitive environment presents challenges to all organizations to effectively leverage all of their competitive weapons. We will look at how many different companies use
the value-profit chain (VPC). In particular, we will look at how two
very different companies, Continental Airlines and SYSCO Food Corporation, started at very different places to create a competitive advantage by using the VPC approach.

Continental is a highly centralized business, in a union environment,
with a high proportion of fixed costs, and significant costs (such as for
fuel and airport fees) that are not completely within the company's
control. Continental chose to focus on people in a "third-time's-a-
charm" effort to avoid bankruptcy and make the airline profitable.
SYSCO Corporation is a decentralized business that comprises over
160 independent operating companies, in both union- and non-union
environments, with a lower proportion of fixed costs and with fewer
costs that are not within the individual companies' control. SYSCO
focused on people to improve its already profitable operations. In spite
of these differences, both companies used the basic Value-Profit Chain
principles to raise their operational and financial performance.

Continental Airlines: From Bankruptcy to Turnaround

In 1994, the need for major change at Continental was obvious. After having emerged from bankruptcy twice in a decade, the airline was again almost bankrupt. Its debt load was oppressive, and it had operated at a loss every year since 1978. Ten chief executive officers (CEOs) had come and gone in ten years, leaving a situation where no consistent strategy existed and no company vision was evident. There was no consensus within the organization as to why a customer would fly Continental instead of a competitor. Operations suffered without a strategy to guide these critical elements of the business.

By nature, international airlines are centralized businesses. When an aircraft flies from Houston to Paris, the operations in those cities have to be identical. Without centralized procedures, operations would be chaotic and confusing to everybody—especially customers. This was exactly the case with Continental. A lack of standardization in operations and procedures had taken a toll on service. Consequently, the company ranked at the bottom of every category tracked by the United States Department of Transportation (DOT), including on-time performance and baggage handling (Figure 1-1). The only category in which Continental "excelled" was customer complaints.

The customer complaints were quite justified. Management seemingly paid no attention to customers, and Continental employees almost went out of their way to be discourteous to customers. The organization promised nothing to the customer, and the employees delivered on that promise. In fact, when executives at Bain & Company, a global consulting firm, were deciding between Houston and Dallas as a location for the company's new offices, they chose Dallas just so that they would not have to fly Continental.

As bad as the customer satisfaction statistics were, Continental's customer-value proposition far exceeded its employee-value proposition. The nature of jobs in the airline industry is quite different from

Building Profit through Building People

Figure 1-1. The Bleak Situation at Continental

most. Unionized workforces with company seniority policies create golden handcuffs that bind employees to the firm economically but not emotionally. For instance, a pilot with fifteen years' experience flying for Continental might hate management, his co-workers, and the general work environment—but going to another airline would not be an option unless he was willing to take a 60% pay cut. This situation creates dissatisfied employees who are stuck in unfulfilling jobs and who are likely to take out their frustrations on customers, management, and co-workers.

It appeared that Continental had done everything possible to create a dissatisfied workforce. The work environment was very class conscious, and executive suites were kept separate from the other employee areas through tight security and vigilance. Functions were compartmentalized. The work environment was hostile after years of contentious labor-management disputes. Layoffs, wage freezes, and pay cuts had created significant distrust for years. In addition, the company had never been able to effectively integrate its earlier mergers and acquisitions with New York Air, PeopleExpress, and Eastern Airlines. At one point, the large bulk of employees referred to themselves as "Eastern" or "PeopleExpress" workers, and only new hires called themselves "Continental" employees. The workforce was fragmented, with employees often pitted against one another by management. (Better they fight among themselves than having them all gang up on management!) Senior management had no compelling vision except to stay afloat. Lower-level managers sought only to collect their paychecks without suffering through explosions among the workers. It was as if the captain had just announced, "The plane is going down! It's every man for himself!"

Continental's employees were good people who wanted to do a good job, but they were shell-shocked after so many years of failure. The revolving door through which so many CEOs entered and departed made it impossible for the staff to become engaged in any mission, vision, or strategy for their company. Continental's managers saw the employees as necessary physical assets but little more. Employees were not recognized for their crucial roles in satisfying customers and helping the business grow. The only clear focus was cutting costs, and in the airline industry labor is the biggest controllable cost. There was inconsistent leadership, lack of a compelling vision, and employees who felt undervalued. Considering this situation, no one was surprised that Continental employees' hearts had hardened.

Everything changed, though. In the span of a single year, Continental's performance turned around in a way seldom observed in the history of any corporation. Continental's revenues grew and netted a $390 million dollar swing in profits. The stock soared, as did its performance on most DOT performance categories. Table 1-1 shows Continental's business overview in 1994, the year before Continental implemented the "Go Forward" plan and adopted the value-profit chain philosophy. In 1995, after the plan was put in place, Continental

Table 1-1. Continental's Business Overview

Metric	1994	1995
Revenues	$5 billion	$5.3 billion
Earnings	($165 million loss)	$225 million profit
Employee Compensation	10th percentile	50th percentile
Stock Price (Per Share)	$6.50	$40.50
On-Time Performance Rank	Last	First
Profit-Sharing Expenses	0	$50 million
Managerial Training	0	100% of managers trained

Continental's success story began in 1995 when the "Go Forward" plan was implemented. All data are from Continental's Annual Reports.

achieved significant improvements in all key metrics including profitability, on-time performance, stock price, and employee rewards.

This positive trend continues. Today Continental is still viewed as one of the premier U.S. airlines in terms of delivering both superior customer service and value to shareholders. It is the fifth-largest airline in the United States and the leading U.S. airline serving Mexico, Central America, and the Western Pacific. For three years in a row (1996–1998) Continental Airlines was ranked as the number two "Most Admired U.S. Airline" by *Fortune* and was number fifty-five on *Fortune's* "100 Best Companies to Work For" for four consecutive years (1996–1999). Perhaps most impressive, Continental consistently has ranked first or second in the DOT ratings for on-time performance and baggage handling, and it was the first company ever to leap from last to first place in J.D. Power and Associates' Frequent Traveler Satisfaction Survey for domestic long-haul flights. The company's stock was trading below $10 a share in 1994; by 2001 it was trading above $50 per share. Despite being hit hard after 9/11, Continental continues to be healthier than many other domestic airlines.

It is a story for the record books and proof positive that a focus on people pays off in real profits. Let's look now at a very different company with similar results based on a people-driven approach.

SYSCO: Building on Initial Success

SYSCO Corporation has had a happier history. The largest marketer and distributor of food service products in North America, the company has been a success from day one. Founded in 1970 by John Baugh and eight other entrepreneurs, it has achieved consistent, double-digit annual growth for more than three decades. SYSCO stocks the kitchens of 420,000 customers ranging from independent restaurants to 3,000 Wendy's restaurants to the Hilton chain of hotels and other hotels, hospitals, colleges, and universities. In 2004 it achieved nearly $30 billion in revenues with sales growth of 12% and profit growth of 16%. SYSCO has 157 distribution locations throughout North America and has consistently outperformed its competitors in the food service industry by two to three times.

This success has been driven by a consistent focus on delivering high-quality products and service to customers and building an organizational culture of entrepreneurial spirit. To create this entrepreneurial spirit, the company organizes around businesses that are small, local, and autonomous. One guiding principle from the beginning was the concept of "earned autonomy," which confers freedom for businesses to focus on the needs of their local markets, without constraints from the corporate headquarters. Thus, business-unit presidents are free to manage their businesses and their workforces however they see fit (within ethical and legal guidelines, of course). Since the mid-1990's when SYSCO began implementing value-profit chain principles, good things have been coming even more quickly. The company closed fiscal year 2001 with a record-breaking 32% net earnings growth and 13% sales growth. By continuously improving its focus on associate and customer satisfaction, the company has some of the happiest shareholders you'll ever come across.

The company's success has caught the attention of just about every major business publication. In 2003 SYSCO was ranked by *Fortune* as number one in its industry in profits, profits as a percentage of assets, profits as a percentage of revenues, ten-year earnings-per-share growth, and ten-year total return to shareholders. From 1998 to 2003, *Forbes* named SYSCO a Platinum 400 company based on its profitability over a one-year and a five-year period. *Business Week* ranked SYSCO number one in the Food and Drug Retailing Industry in its 2003 performance ranking. And in 2004 Emory University's Edward Hess identified four *Fortune* 100 companies that displayed strong organic growth (i.e., not through acquisitions) over the past five years. SYSCO was one of those four.

The Common Thread: The Value-Profit Chain

We have two very different companies beginning at dramatically different starting points; one was in bankruptcy and one had a history of solid performance. Both companies achieved the same result—strong financial and operational performance and committed employees. What is the common thread? It's the value-profit chain (VPC). The value-profit chain extends the basic service-profit chain developed by Heskett, Sasser, and Schlesinger (1997) to firms that do more than just provide services (Heskett, Sasser, & Schlesinger, 2005).

Both Continental and SYSCO have profited from the vision and understanding of the value-profit chain. They have put it into practice with outstanding results. We focus on these two companies for two reasons. First, we look to them because they demonstrate unarguable success and illustrate the power of the principles underlying the value-profit chain. Second, these firms are ones where we have personal experience. Ken Carrig has experienced the success from the inside and knows details in each case. Ken was vice president of global human resources (HR) at Continental from 1995 to 1998; presently he serves as the executive vice president of administration at SYSCO Corporation. Patrick Wright has studied both these companies in his role as a researcher, and he acted as a sounding board for Ken as he led the administration function within the organizations.

Let's see how the value-profit chain's basic principles led to the turnaround at Continental and accelerated growth at SYSCO.

Continental's Turnaround

Continental Airlines' chairman and CEO Gordon Bethune wrote a book, *From Worst to First: Behind the Scenes of Continental's Remarkable Comeback*, about Continental's amazing turnaround in the 1990s (Bethune, 1998). In it, he stresses the importance of making employees happy so they can make customers happy so they can make shareholders happy.

Continental's turnaround, beginning in 1995, is a dramatic example of the results that can be achieved by leveraging the VPC. The implementation of effective management practices based on the philosophy of the value-profit chain—even after a decade of management failures—was the main driver in an amazing turnaround that no one could have predicted. Before long, the new management practices at Continental had transformed the attitudes and work habits of the entire workforce. And once that transformation was complete, customers could not help but notice—and respond. The list of eventual winners at Continental included the associates, customers, and shareholders who, bruised and battered though they were, had hung on through the lean years until the transformation was complete.

At the base of this turnaround was the "Go Forward" plan. This plan articulated a consistent strategy with regard to customers, shareholders, operations, and employees. It had the following components.

- "Fund the Future" focused on developing the financial discipline and performance to eliminate an oppressive debt load and deliver profitability to shareholders.

- "Fly to Win" stood for the proposition that Continental would eliminate routes that continually lost money and focus resources on routes where they could make money.
- "Make Reliability a Reality" was a promise to customers and focused on delivering a consistent, high-quality customer experience.
- "Working Together" described a new culture for employees at Continental. It articulated the beginning of an employee-value proposition that would engage employees emotionally as well as economically.

We will describe the specifics of Continental's "Go Forward" plan later, particularly as it was executed through a whole new set of management practices. For now, though, here are the basic VPC principles that this strategy exemplified.

- First, it articulated a customer-value proposition: *We will provide consistent, safe, high-quality service.* This is a compelling reason for people to want to fly on Continental. It was this delivery of an outcome valued by customers (consistent, high-quality service) that would drive the revenues needed to be profitable. For the first time, the organization focused on driving revenues through customer service, rather than simply engaging in another round of massive cost cuts that hurt customers as much as employees. In fact, one of Bethune's most famous quotations is, "You know, you can make a pizza so cheap that no one will buy it."
- Second, it articulated an employee-value proposition: *We will provide a winning work environment.* This is a compelling reason for Continental employees to both come to work and, once there, deliver a positive customer experience. The goal was to create a work environment where people could see how their individual and team performance could influence others: co-workers, customers, and shareholders. Success would be contagious. As employees succeeded, they would want more success, and experience an attractive

work environment which would draw them back daily. Again, this was summed up by Bethune, "I've never seen a successful organization where people didn't want to come to work each day."

SYSCO's Acceleration

SYSCO's performance has been consistently solid (Figure 1-2). It has always had a strong customer-value proposition focused on delivering the right products at the right time to meet customer needs. Nevertheless, in recent years, this company has demonstrated that focusing on associates and customers can lead to even better performance that consistently outperforms its industry.

The million-dollar question is "So, why is SYSCO so successful?" Business analysts note things such as sales mix and use of technology, size, healthy cash-flow, brand recognition, warehousing efficiencies, and wide geographic reach.

Figure 1-2. SYSCO's Sales and Earnings

28+ Years of Sales and Earnings Increases!

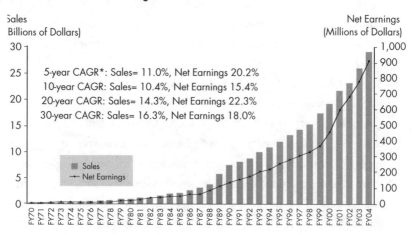

5-year CAGR*: Sales= 11.0%, Net Earnings 20.2%
10-year CAGR: Sales= 10.4%, Net Earnings 15.4%
20-year CAGR: Sales= 14.3%, Net Earnings 22.3%
30-year CAGR: Sales= 16.3%, Net Earnings 18.0%

Building Profit through Building People

Those statements are all true, but here's a differing view from the authors, who have seen the ins and outs of the company: "It's all about people." The driver of these business-strengthening strategies is people. The analysts have recognized this focus on people noting recruitment and retention of a well-trained sales staff, investing in the sales force, entrepreneurial management structure, and high quality customer service.

Food service is a low-margin business where top-line growth is hard to come by—so shareholder value is created mostly by generating higher returns to shareholders. The most popular approach to generate these returns is by cutting operational costs through gains in operational efficiency. Of course there are benefits of scale, but size is not the only key to consistent success.

The next chapter provides solid evidence of why it is all about people. SYSCO has one of the highest (86%) associate retention rates in the industry, and this factor directly impacts its standing in the marketplace. This people-related facet of business may not be the first thing considered if the focus is on growth, but we think it's the proverbial elephant in the room.

The impact of customer "churn" (turnover) or lack of customer loyalty on the revenue growth and cost of the operations is a less frequently considered factor. An illustration of the significance of customers is that in some service companies, reducing customer churn by 50% can increase earnings before interest and taxes by 3% by year four, and those gains are compounded by the perpetuity effects of this additional revenue. This is real impact. Reducing the customer churn or increasing customer loyalty can result in measurable difference for companies in low-margin industries. It is about people. Not plots on graphs or pricey plans from consultants—but about performance through people.

Why is an organization's workforce critical to the customer retention equation? Customer loyalty and operational excellence are affected by a satisfied, productive, and committed workforce. High associate retention cuts the cost of operations. SYSCO, where good management practices have always been part of the culture, is an excellent example of what happens when things go right from the very beginning. The basic principle espoused out by John Baugh when he established SYSCO was "the importance of taking care of all constituents, associates, customers, communities, suppliers and shareholders." The emphasis was on associates (the sales force) because committed associates drive the satisfaction of all other constituents. Employee satisfaction has been underscored with the implementation of a rigorous set of programs inspired by VPC thinking. As associate satisfaction has increased, so has the company's customer retention, and as customer retention has increased, so has profitability. The result is greater portfolio value for shareholders.

Overview

Satisfied associates drive customer loyalty. Sounds pretty simple, doesn't it? Well, if the strategy were that simple, there would be countless examples of companies with high retention rates and stunning customer satisfaction. What's the catch? The strategy must be executed with excellence and innovation. These tenets—customers, employees, excellence in execution, and innovation—form the basis of the VPC philosophy.

Although the principles guiding both Continental and SYSCO are the same, the details are quite different. As we move forward in this book, we will share with you the ins and outs of implementing this vision based on our experience in these two totally different environments. Our specific examples will come from SYSCO. In fact, we will provide you with some of the actual tools that the company used and continues to use to fuel its growth. You can implement the VPC using the approach and tools offered in this book, regardless of the size or type of your company, the product or service you offer, or the state of your balance sheet.

RECAP:

It is all about people. Two completely different firms transformed themselves by leveraging and integrating human resources practices, people, processes, and customer service.

CHAPTER 2

The Value-Profit Chain Redefined

In the previous chapter, we discussed two examples of companies that have used VPC thinking to drive vastly improved business performance. Although value-profit chain thinking is not new, most people have only a general, and sometimes overly simplistic, understanding of it.

Even among those who are more knowledgeable about the VPC, much of the past writing has focused almost exclusively on driving customer satisfaction to improve business profitability. We do not disagree with this notion, but over the years we have come to conclude that customer satisfaction is only the final step in one mechanism through which skilled, committed employees can drive increased profits. To know how employees influence customer satisfaction, one has to know what first makes a customer satisfied.

In this chapter we describe how our experience has influenced our view of the VPC and how the power behind it can help your business improve. Let's first look at the evolution of the VPC.

The Service-Profit Chain

In 1994, James Heskett and several of his colleagues at the Harvard Business School published a seminal article, "Putting the Service Profit Chain to Work" (Heskett, 1994), including an illustration of the chain (Figure 2-1). They stated that service-industry companies could enhance their profitability by improving their employee satisfaction. Working backward from profit, the authors noted the following:

1. In the service industry, the costs of acquiring new customers can be exceedingly high. The surest route to a profitable enterprise comes from customer loyalty.
2. Customers will remain loyal only as long as they remain satisfied.
3. A firm builds customer satisfaction by consistently delivering valuable services to its customers.
4. In service industries, exceptional value is created by innovative, loyal, and productive associates.
5. Satisfied employees are productive employees, and employee satisfaction can be enhanced through effective management practices.

There is no doubt that loyal customers are the most profitable ones. In addition, no one argues with the fact that satisfied employees serve cus-

Figure 2-1. The Classic Service-Profit Chain

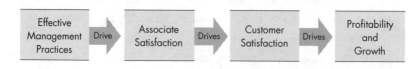

Adapted with permission from "Putting the Service Profit Chain to Work," J.L. Heskett, T.O. Jones, G.W. Loveman, W.E. Sasser, Jr., and L.A. Schlesinger, *Harvard Business Review*, (March–April 1994), 164-174.

Building Profit through Building People

tomers better. In fact a number of research studies over the years have consistently demonstrated support for the link between employee satisfaction and customer satisfaction (Rafaeli, 1989; Rogg, Schmidt, Shull, & Schmitt, 2001; Schlesinger & Zornitsky, 1991; Schmit & Allscheid, 1985; Schneider, & Bowen, 1985; Schneider, White, & Paul, 1998). But what *really* drives customer satisfaction? What do satisfied employees do that *leads* to customer satisfaction? What *specific practices* can management develop and implement to increase the satisfaction of employees? These are questions that are crucial but often left unexplored by firms thinking about implementing value-profit chain principles.

We propose a slight modification to the original service-profit chain: a model with a more descriptive explanation of the process of creating customer value with a broader influence than in just the service sector (Figure 2-2).

Figure 2-2. The Modified Service-Profit Chain

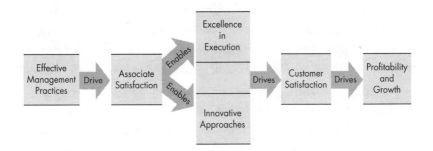

The Value-Profit Chain

A firm with a loyal, motivated workforce is not assured of superior profits. Instead, satisfied associates allow companies to:

1. Develop excellence in execution of routine tasks. This ability to perform routine tasks better than the competition is critical to superior customer satisfaction. Then the positive energy generated in the organization as a result of satisfied employees needs to be channeled toward improving systems, processes, and service. These improvements can then contribute to achieving higher customer satisfaction.
2. Develop innovative approaches to capture business opportunities. Often, the stumbling block to successful implementation of new processes or initiatives is employee resistance. A satisfied, motivated workforce is more likely to generate workplace innovations and is more receptive to proposed workplace innovations than a less satisfied workforce.

A satisfied workforce enables a company to pursue excellence in execution and develop innovative approaches. Only then can customers be satisfied. The company's management needs to put in place infrastructure, systems, and processes that will initiate and sustain excellence and innovation, which are the principal components of an effective VPC.

This expansion of the model makes complete sense, yet it still may not provide enough detail for firms to actually tailor VPC logic to their particular strategy. Consequently, we will expand upon this basic logic to provide more specific guidance. Let's explore these concepts in more detail to help you consider how VPC thinking can help you improve your organization.

Take a look at our VPC model (Figure 2-3). We have added underpinnings, if you will, to demonstrate our expanded view. We will start our discussion at the revenue versus cost side of the model and work our way back to the most important: people.

Figure 2-3. The Value-Profit Chain

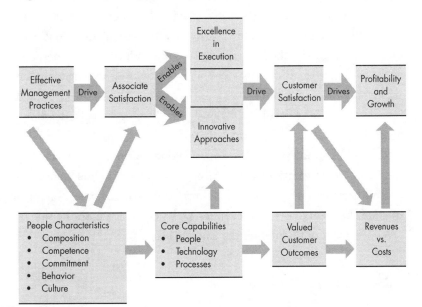

Revenues versus Costs: What Drives Your Profits?

We begin with a basic, yet important assumption: A firm's profits are equal to its revenues minus its costs (substantive and detailed accounting issues notwithstanding). Although this is not profound, understanding the relative weight a firm puts on the revenue or cost factors is critical to determining how it will execute the VPC.

For instance, consider Delta Air Lines (Brannigan & Lisser 1996; Brannigan & White, 1997). Up until 1994, Delta's entire strategy revolved around revenues. It sought to (and did) provide the best customer service in the industry. This was delivered by having highly paid, internally developed, extremely committed and experienced employees who knew what customers wanted and provided it. Delta's cost structure was the highest in the industry, but that did not matter because the company's value proposition revolved around charging premium prices for its high-quality service. In other words, its focus was on the revenue side of the equation. On the other hand, Continental was striving to be the low-cost option among the major airlines. The goal was to drive down costs by breaking unions, holding tight on wages, minimizing training, and not worrying about turnover and repeated rounds of layoffs. Obviously, the strategy revolved around focusing on the cost side of the equation.

Emphasizing one part of the equation does not necessitate ignoring the other. Delta wanted to raise revenues and Continental wanted to control costs. However, when decisions came that required making a trade-off between costs and revenues, Delta came down on the side of revenues and Continental on the side of costs.

Valued Customer Outcomes

Strongly related to the revenue-cost balance is the question of "What valued customer outcomes does the organization seek to fulfill?" The answers to this critical strategic question drive almost everything else in VPC thinking.

This is not to say that outcomes other than high priority ones are irrelevant, but rather that every business needs to prioritize its own outcomes. A company probably can deliver exceptionally well on just one or a very few customer outcomes and accept that on others it may deliver on par or even below the level of its competitors. When considering valued customer outcomes, one looks not for product or service attributes, but rather for the underlying customer needs that are being met. For instance, for decades Caterpillar Inc.'s worldwide distribution capability provided it with the ability to get customers needed parts for its heavy equipment within 24 hours anywhere in the world. This provided a long-term competitive advantage until Komatsu America Corp. began to steal customers with their high quality machines. In other words, the valued customer outcome was not the service capability to get a part for a broken down machine (Caterpillar) but uptime for the machine, which could also be met by having a machine that does not break down (Komatsu) (Bartlett & Rangan, 1985).

Core Capabilities: People, Technology, and Processes

To deliver any set of valued customer outcomes, a firm has to develop a core capability. Although this term often is misunderstood or defined differently in different sources, we define a "core capability" as a group of people using a particular technology (or technologies) in a set of business processes to create a set of valued customer outcomes.

Now, this may seem to run counter to our earlier principle, "It's all about people." But, of course, success cannot be achieved just by bringing in really good people but not equipping them with technology or processes. "It's all about people" means that people are the ultimate source of long-term competitive advantage. In today's world, technology is easily copied by competitors, and so it seldom provides any long-term competitive advantage. Similarly, competitors can usually imitate most basic business processes, so these do not likely result in sustainable advantages. However, a highly skilled and committed workforce is difficult to imitate.

Just as people without technology or processes add little value to the business, even more it is even truer that technology and processes without people are completely without value. It is people who design and execute processes. It is people who design, work with, and leverage technology.

So, in examining the VPC, we need to recognize the technology and processes as important enablers but realize that the critical elements to success are the people. What about people makes a difference? Read on.

People Characteristics

The crucial characteristics needed in an organization's people depend somewhat on the actual valued outcomes that the business seeks to deliver. But, in general, we can describe the important people characteristics along four dimensions: composition, competence, commitment, and behavior.

- *Composition* is the mix of skills and demographic characteristics the firm needs.
- *Competence* is the knowledge, skills, abilities, and other characteristics of people in key jobs.
- *Commitment* is the emotional engagement that employees feel to the firm.
- *Behavior* is the things that employees must actually do in order for the firm to be successful.

Let's examine a business in which valued outcomes influence the types of people found within the organization.

Starbucks has revolutionized the coffee drinking habits of people around the world. Its growth rate is phenomenal; it opens approximately 2 stores every business day and hires 200 people each day. Starbucks has grown from a single store to a five-billion-dollar company operating over 6,132 stores in the United States and an additional 2,437 in 33 other countries (Starbucks 2004 Annual Report). Its profits have risen at about a 25% annual rate and its stock has increased more than 2000% since 1992.

The secret to this success is described by Chairman Howard Schultz who states "Great companies are linked to a unique relationship with their people. Those people are linked to a unique relationship to their customers." (Holmes, Bennett, Carlisle, & Dawson, 2002.) Let's look at the four people characteristics at Starbucks.

Composition. The composition of Starbucks people represents a diversity of backgrounds seldom found in other companies. The U.S.

Building Profit through Building People

workforce consists of 63% women and 24% people of color, while the executive ranks include 31% women and 13% people of color. However, the diversity extends beyond racial/gender characteristics. The 2004 Corporate Social Responsibility Report states "At Starbucks the term diversity includes factors such as age, race, gender, sexual orientation, national origin, physical and mental attributes, education, skills, experiences, and ideas. When we apply our collective mixture of differences and similarities in pursuit of business goals, then great things happen."

Competence. While many retailers and fast food companies rely on a low skill, high turnover commodity-type workforce, Starbucks prides itself on the quality of its people. States Schultz "We've never viewed our people as commodities. We view our people as business partners." (In fact, Starbucks refers to employees as "partners.") This partnership exemplifies itself through Starbucks' passion for service and consistency. Each new employee attends a series of indoctrination seminars to learn about being a "barista." These seminars include Brewing the Perfect Cup, a class that emphasizes the complex nomenclature (e.g. "triple-tall nonfat mocha") and the rules that must be followed (e.g. "Milk must be steamed to at least 150 degrees F, but never more than 170 degrees F. Every espresso shot must be pulled within 23 seconds or tossed.") In addition, the company builds competence in its partners in the areas of retail skills, coffee knowledge, customer service, leadership, and communications. In other words, Starbucks seeks highly competent partners who can provide a consistently high-quality customer experience

Commitment. Commitment is central to the ability of a company to distinguish itself from competitors, and Starbucks exemplifies this attribute. Its mission statement's first objective is "Provide a great work environment and treat each other with respect and dignity." Underlying this objective is the belief that if people relate to the company they work for, form an emotional tie to it, and buy into its dreams then they will pour their hearts into making it better.

Commitment can take two forms: People may just want to remain with the firm or they may want to truly contribute to the firm's success. Starbucks' partners certainly choose to stay with the company. Annual employee turnover is 60% compared with 140% for hourly workers in the fast-food business generally. Some baristas have been with Starbucks seven or more years. In addition, these partners truly want to contribute. In 2005, Starbucks earned its rank of 11th on *Fortune's* 100 Top Companies to Work For list. In 2003 82% of the partners said that they were satisfied or very satisfied and 73% reported a high level of engagement (Starbucks Corporate Social Responsibility Report, 2004). This satisfaction and engagement result in partners who are committed to the firm's success. One partner describes this commitment as "We literally take apart almost every machine in the store after closing. I have a 1969 Camaro that I keep in show condition, and I don't spend as much time detailing it as I do the espresso machine, but I will not stop until it is clean. I'm into it."

Behavior. Behavior involves creating a line-of-sight so that employees are well aware of how their activities and behaviors contribute to the firm's performance. First, the partners must exhibit behaviors that generate the unique Starbucks' customer experience. They must exhibit the friendly, helpful attitude that makes Starbucks that "Third Place" between home and work where customers gather. They must follow the rules for providing a consistent high quality product.

Second, the behaviors are what keep Starbucks in a constant state of renewal. In fact, many of Starbucks' fastest growing products stemmed from the suggestions of partners. The idea of a cold-coffee, blended beverage was the collective brainchild of a few partners. And when one of the store managers began experimenting with customized in-store music tapes, the idea evolved into the latest Starbucks branded CD's (Schultz & Yang, 1997).

In essence, people characteristics relevant to an organization's success go beyond just associate satisfaction. Firms have to develop people with the right competencies and the right composition so that (1) employees will be satisfied, and (2) this satisfaction will lead to behaviors that lead to the organization's success. Firms build core capabilities by building the right people characteristics and providing employees with the right technologies and processes.

Culture and Values

Finally, any discussion of building an organization based on VPC thinking would be incomplete without recognizing the importance of culture and values. Culture is an often cited but ill-defined concept used to explain organizational behavioral patterns—and success or failure. We define culture as the shared values, norms, and expected ways of behaving that create a common frame of reference for all organizational members.

Culture's importance is seen in many ways. First, culture is often integrally woven into the business model. What would Southwest Airlines' business model look like without its fun culture? What would Microsoft's business model look like without its competitive and innovative culture? Second, culture often provides the decision-making framework that individuals need when standard management practices are not apparent. Every day, employees face situations for which they may not have received formal training or guidance and they are forced to make decisions about how to respond. Culture provides the guidance for responding the "right" way—the way the company wants them to. Finally, culture determines the effectiveness of management practices by providing a framework for decision-making that ultimately affects both employees and customers. In this way culture infiltrates the entire business model to provide a foundation for aligning all the parts toward organizational effectiveness.

We will provide some best-practice management practices in the following chapters. But, consider yourself warned: Some of them simply will not work if the culture is not right. For instance, in the early 1990's, the pharmaceutical company Merck & Co. instituted gainsharing in some of its manufacturing facilities with tremendous results. However, facilities at other companies, using the same gainsharing processes, saw little or no success. Why the difference? Merck's culture had promoted trust between managers and employees; therefore, a gainsharing plan was interpreted by employees as a way for them to share in the company's success. In firms where culture of trust did not exist, the employees viewed gainsharing as a way for management to exploit them.

Does the Value-Profit Chain Really Work?

This is a fair question. Several studies over the past eight years have demonstrated support for different aspects of the VPC. The bulk of this research has focused on the relationship between management practices and profitability.

For example, in 1995 Mark Huselid found that corporations that had implemented high performance work systems (HPWS, a set of management practices aimed at building a skilled and motivated workforce) saw significantly higher profits and market values than firms that were lower in their level of HPWS. His results have been replicated in studies of certain industries (auto assembly plants by MacDuffie, 1995; banks by Delery & Doty, 1996; companies in New Zealand by Guthrie, 2001). These studies demonstrate that, on average, a one standard deviation increase in these management practices was associated with a 20% increase in profitability.

These academic studies tend to mirror the results found in the popular literature. For instance, *Fortune* magazine conducts an annual assessment of the "100 Best Companies to Work For." If satisfied associates fuel corporate profits, one would expect the 100 best employers

Figure 2-4. Average Annual Return to Shareholders

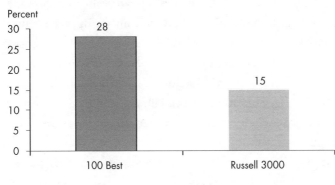

Percent

Fortune Magazine 100 Best Companies, 2004
Russell 3000 Index, 2004

to outperform average firms—and they do, as shown on the Russell 3000 Index, an indexed investment fund of the 3000 top-performing U.S. stocks (Figure 2-4).

Fulmer, Gerhart, and Scott (2003) compared the performance of *Fortune* magazine's "100 Best Companies to Work For" with (a) a matched set of peer companies from each member's industry, and (b) a value-weighted index of firms from the NYSE/AMEX/NASDAQ stock listings over a six-year time frame including the three years preceding the announcement of their status on the list and the three years following. They found that the 100 Best Companies outperformed their comparison groups in 1997 and 1998. In addition, the 100 Best Companies outperformed their comparison groups on the cumulative returns from 1995–1997.

Watson Wyatt, a management consulting firm, also reported similar results from the research on its Human Capital Index®, a set of practices that Watson Wyatt identified as being related to firm performance. They found that firms in the highest quartile of their index saw a five-year (1996–2001) return to shareholders of 64% compared to only 21% among the firms in the bottom quartile (Watson Wyatt, 2001).

Although these studies have focused on the relationship between the boxes at each end of the VPC model, research also supports the links in between. For instance, SYSCO periodically conducts customer surveys and marketing associate satisfaction surveys. There has consistently been a strong predictive correlation between marketing associate satisfaction and customer satisfaction at each division. Every 18 months SYSCO collects customer, work climate, and business results and correlates them to verify that the associations among these measures remain true.

The linkage is telling. These figures show year after year that companies with satisfied employees are also the ones that deliver the best overall results (Figure 2-5). And companies that score high on employee satisfaction consistently receive the highest scores from their customers (Table 2-1).

Figure 2-5. Customer Satisfaction Reflects Employee Satisfaction, FY 2005, SYSCO Companies

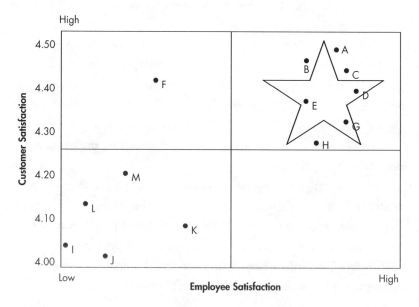

Building Profit through Building People

Table 2-1. Satisfied Employees Deliver Better Results, FY 2005, SYSCO Companies

	High	←		→	Low
Associate Satisfaction Score	4.00–5.00	3.90–3.99	3.75–3.89	3.55–3.74	<3.55
Customer Loyalty Score	4.55	4.40	4.25	4.15	4.05
Retention, Marketing Associates	88%	85%	83%	82.5%	82.3%
Retention, Drivers	87%	81%	81%	75%	76%

Another company that focuses on the relationship between employee satisfaction, customer satisfaction, and investor satisfaction is Sears, Roebuck & Co. (Sears). Faced with the rise of new competitors such as Wal-Mart on the low end and specialty retailers such as Gap, or Home Depot, Sears' performance began to flounder. The old Sears model of combining catalog shopping and large mall-based retail outlets did not seem to differentiate Sears in a way that was sustainable.

Sears' turnaround began in 1992, when the company redefined its mission in terms of the "3C's": "a Compelling place to shop, a Compelling place to work, and a Compelling place to invest." Employee satisfaction was a critical ingredient.

Sears conducts detailed measurement of its employees' satisfaction and looks for correlations. Figure 2-6 shows the correlations that Sears has found.

Overview

The research literature has demonstrated the positive association of human resource practices with employee attitudes as well as various

Figure 2-6. Customer Satisfaction Reflects Employee Satisfaction, FY 2005, SYSCO Companies

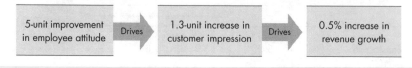

Reprinted with permission from "The Employee-Customer-Profit Chain at Sears." Anthony J. Rucci; Steven P. Kirn, and Richard T. Quinn, *Harvard Business Review,* January 1, 1998.

measures of employee, operational, and financial performance. These relationships support the underlying logic of the VPC. Therefore, organizations that build a committed, interested, and engaged workforce can gain a true competitive advantage.

Regardless of this evidence, the VPC still is far from being universally accepted or embraced. Why?

The VPC philosophy is not difficult to grasp, but it is difficult to execute consistently and effectively over the long term. And excellence and innovation in execution are critical. According to a national Gallup poll, over 70% of employees surveyed in the United States are not fully interested in their work (The Gallup Organization, 2001).

Even though the VPC model might seem simplistic or trivial, it has been rarely implemented properly as indicated by so many people being dissatisfied and unhappy in their jobs. Many organizational success stories reveal that credible, capable leadership is a common key factor in building a satisfied workforce. This book will not only detail the leadership skills required to build organization-wide commitment to the VPC vision, but also will highlight the important links between systems and success measures.

Building Profit through Building People

RECAP:

1. The value-profit chain tells us that effective management practices go hand in hand with employee satisfaction.
2. All things being equal, organizations with happy and committed employees outperform those with less happy and less committed employees.
3. Focusing on the value-profit chain can build loyalty among associates and customers and can lead to increased profitability and growth.
4. Tailoring value-profit chain logic to a particular firm entails consideration of the relative importance of revenues versus costs, the valued customer outcomes the firm provides, the core capabilities used to deliver those outcomes, the people characteristics necessary, and the culture and values of the firm.

CHAPTER 3

Your Customer: A Critical Link in the Value-Profit Model

The premise of the value-profit chain (VPC) is that customer satisfaction and customer retention are accurate predictors of a firm's profitability. Two questions immediately arise:

1. Should a firm strive to retain *all* its customers?
2. How can a firm manage customer satisfaction?

The answer to these questions can determine the success or failure of any product or service business. In this chapter, we lay out a three-step process that can build the understanding of your business and initiate the move toward increased profits:

1. Identify your most profitable customers.
2. Determine what those customers need.
3. Deliver those services expertly and reliably.

To illustrate, let's first examine in a general way how Continental, SYSCO, and other companies have handled customer satisfaction. Then, we will examine in some detail how SYSCO has established a process for prospecting, developing, and satisfying the most profitable customers.

Continental and Delta

As discussed in the opening of Chapter 2, until 1994 the strategy of Delta Air Lines was to maximize revenues by providing the best customer service in the industry. Highly paid employees delivered that service. Delta's costs were high, but the airline charged premium prices for such high-quality service. In other words, the focus was on the revenue side of the equation. This emphasis gave them particular sway over the business traveler, who provides the most profits. Our illustration of this basic business model is in Figure 3-1.

At the other end of the airport, Continental was striving to be the low-cost airline among the major carriers by keeping a tight rein on costs, including those of training and wages. Obviously, Continental's strategy emphasized lowering the cost side of the equation. These low costs were not as important to business travelers as other factors. Our presentation of Continental's basic business model is in Figure 3-2.

So these airlines were implementing business models that served different customers. Delta's focused on the most profitable customer while Continental's sought to aim at the mass market.

As revealed in the airlines' initial market strategies, companies can arrive at dramatically different places when it comes to valued customer outcomes. This is not to say that any set of outcomes is necessarily bet-

Figure 3-1. Delta's Pre-1994 Business Model

Building Profit through Building People

ter than another, but rather that every organization needs to set priorities for the various outcomes because it is impossible to excel at delivering all outcomes. A company must recognize that for some outcomes it may only deliver as well as (or even less well) than its competitors.

Why is this purposeful focus crucial? Well, note what happened during the mid-1990's. Delta was in financial trouble, laden with debt, and faced with the discount carrier ValuJet competing out of its main Atlanta hub. Delta began cutting costs. Most significantly it cut costs by laying off its most critical resource: skilled, experienced, and committed employees. As contingent and inexperienced employees began taking over, operations faltered, leading to decreased on-time performance, long lines, increased baggage handling mistakes, and growth in customer complaints. Clearly the strategy resulted in its failure to reliably deliver on the outcomes most valuable to Delta's core customer, the business traveler. Consequently, it soon lost their customer's loyalty as well as their business (Brannigan & Lisser, 1996; Brannigan & White, 1997).

During the latter part of the 1990's, according to Delta's annual reports, the company's revenues grew at only 3% a year while the rest of the airline industry's revenues grew at an annual rate of 11%. Consensus among industry analysts revealed the belief that the flat rev-

Figure 3-2. Continental's Pre-1994 Business Model

enues were directly attributable to the airline's loss of business customers. This unfortunate situation created the entirely unanticipated, *de facto* business model that we constructed as Figure 3-3.

Note how this approach differed from Continental's shift in strategy starting in 1995 with the "Go Forward" plan. The "Make Reliability at Reality" plank of the plan focused on delivering high quality, reliable customer service. Continental quickly improved its on-time performance. Baggage handling improved. Special lines were created for business travelers to ensure that they never had to wait in a long line. In fact, at Houston Intercontinental Airport, business travelers could check in at the parking lot. The employees became more satisfied and friendlier simply because it is much easier to be friendly when customers are not frustrated. Continental soon became the most reliable deliverer of the outcomes valued by business travelers and was recognized for these accomplishments when it won the J.D. Power and Associates' award for best airline in 1996 and 1997. Continental did not stop there. It began to offer additional services that

Figure 3-3. Delta's Post-1994, Unanticipated, De Facto Business Model

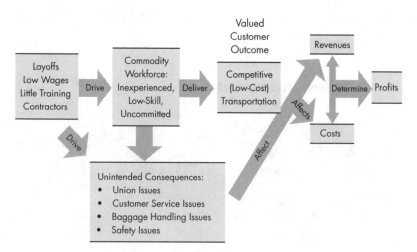

Building Profit through Building People

made it even more pleasurable for its most valuable business customers to fly with the carrier. First, they provided free upgrades to
first class for the most frequent travelers. The overhead storage space
was expanded so that travelers could carry more bags on the plane.
These were simple, low-cost offerings that offered tremendous value
to the most profitable customers. Although some airlines have imitat-
ed them, these changes positioned Continental as a first-mover and
conferred a significant advantage over its competitors.

Identify Good Customers

The first lesson from the story of Continental and Delta is the importance of knowing which customers make money for you. In the airline
industry, companies covet the business traveler, who pays four to five
times more than the leisure traveler. Delta, which had known its customers, made changes that lost that customer. Continental found a way
to capture that same customer and fill a void.

No doubt, it is important to know who your good customers are.
Many have heard the legendary stories of Nordstrom accepting
returned tire chains from a dissatisfied shopper (although Nordstrom
has never sold tire chains) and of a Southwest gate agent using his personal plane to fly a late-arriving passenger to a business meeting. What
is typically lost in these anecdotes is that companies like Nordstrom
and Southwest know who their most valuable customers are. They are
willing to push the limits of service for these customers because they
understand the value of loyal, frequent customers. The customers
receiving this special treatment likely had potential lifetime values of
tens (if not hundreds) of thousands of dollars.

Less celebrated are the occasions when Nordstrom and Southwest
"fire" customers with little lifetime value. At Nordstrom, a well-trained
sales clerk can spot a troublesome but low-potential customer and

suggest other retail establishments that may have what the customer seeks. Southwest's operating model is based on short flight segments and a first-come, first-served advantage for customers who arrive at the gate early. These approaches dissuade the coast-to-coast business flyers, who put a premium on their time. Thus business travelers are prevented from being dissatisfied because they are "fired" through Southwest's practices.

Profitable companies understand that a small fraction of their customer base drives the majority of corporate profits. SYSCO has identified its most profitable customers and concentrates on offering them outstanding service. Broad industry studies conducted by Ernan Roman Direct Marketing suggest that 10% of a firm's customers generate 30% to 50% of the firm's profits. SYSCO's customer stratification analysis proves this point. The top 10% of its customers generates 40% to 50% of the profits.

In SYSCO's case, a good customer does not necessarily mean a large restaurant chain. Small establishments, even mom-and-pop restaurants, are among these best customers. The good customers are those— regardless of size—who rely primarily on the company to supply food, utensils, dishware, cooking equipment, cleaning supplies—pretty much everything needed to operate a successful restaurant.

Determine What Good Customers Want

Having identified the most profitable customer, the next step is to determine what those customers need and want, or in other words "What valued customer outcomes do we seek to fulfill?" The answers to this critical strategic question will drive almost everything else in VPC thinking.

Valued customer outcomes are the crucial dimensions of a product or service that have the greatest impact on customer satisfaction. Using

Building Profit through Building People

the Continental and Delta examples, consider your own business flying experiences. What outcomes do you value? What makes or breaks your customer experience? When you check in, do you want to face long lines? How important is it that you arrive on time to your destination? How critical is it for your bags to arrive with you? When exceptions occur (as they inevitably do), do you want clear answers or "I don't know" answers from customer service agents?

A recent study within the hotel industry attempted to determine what most strongly determines customer satisfaction. By surveying 1,351 customers from 279 hotels, researchers attempted to determine which aspects of the hotel experience best drove customer satisfaction and which employee groups were responsible for providing those satisfaction drivers. The researchers found that front-desk performance (ease in getting the room, friendliness of the front desk staff, etc.) was the most important determinant of the overall satisfaction. Front-desk performance also was the only driver that was potentially able to offset poor performance on other dimensions (Hartline, Woolridge, & Jones, 2003).

Marriott International, Inc.'s own customer surveys reinforce this determinant. Marriott found that 84% of responding customers indicated that the first 10 minutes of guest service were most critical to their satisfaction.

Tied directly to what customers want and to valued-customer outcomes is the need to customize service levels in order to achieve maximum profitability and growth. To provide premium service to discount customers is inefficient. In a competitive market with significant variation in different customers' ability and willingness to pay and in their expectations, firms must link the level of service to the profitability of the customer. Again, the Delta and Continental stories illustrate the importance of this step. In cutting costs, Delta stopped delivering on the basic expectations of its core customer. Continental, on the other hand, customized its service for its core customer. The special check-in lines, boarding priority, generous frequent-flyer program, and cabin upgrades focused specifically on providing a special level of service to the most profitable customers.

Customer satisfaction is achieved by offering high service levels and effectively recovering when service fails. In an ideal world, service levels would be optimal for all customer types, based on the customers' lifetime value. In the real world, however, this decision is made qualitatively. And it is the front-line employees who are in the best position to make this judgment, which is another reason for them to be engaged in and satisfied with their jobs. Additionally, when implementing both superior service levels and failed-service recoveries, there is one common thing—service—that best can be provided by effective and productive employees. Both these points illustrate the importance of the people component in the VPC.

Deliver Services Expertly Reliably

Valued customer outcomes are the outcomes that are most critical for influencing customer satisfaction. Just knowing the outcomes, however, does not help unless you are able to consistently deliver them.

Marriott exemplifies this emphasis on service and reliability in the hotel industry. Having determined that the first ten minutes of experience in the hotel was the most important for customers, Marriott also found that 75% of a desk clerk's time was involved in chores not related to check-in or check-out, and that those chores actually distracted the clerks from providing such service. Consequently, Marriott redesigned the job of the desk clerk to cover a broader set of activities with greater skill requirements. Now, 80% of Marriott properties employ a fully cross-trained "guest service associate" who is paid for acquiring what once were valet, doorman, bellman, concierge, and front-desk skills. Marriott also removed phones from the front desk. As a result of these changes, check-in speed dropped from almost three minutes to just over a minute and a half, with 98% of all check-ins less than two minutes. This redesign also reduced overhead by 40% (Verespej, 1994).

Similarly, SYSCO has spent considerable time, effort, and money to understand its customers and what they want. The company also devotes substantial resources to understanding how well it is delivering those outcomes.

Most people's experiences with restaurants are based on their role as a diner; they go to eat, not to analyze the operation. Restaurant operations may seem quite simple: take the order, prepare the food, and serve it. Behind the scenes, though, these operations are quite complex.

Restaurant managers must ensure that the right amounts of the right mix of foods and materials (napkins, silverware, and so forth) are available every single day. Although every restaurant may have a different price point, all are concerned with costs. Thus, SYSCO's marketing associates have to consult with customers to understand their needs and how the company's product lines can meet those needs in ways that are cost effective for the restaurant. This interaction should result in the managers preparing orders that will enable their restaurants to have adequate stock without incurring undue costs.

Once ordered, products must be delivered on time and accurately. Late or incorrect deliveries can result in excess inventory that spoils, or inadequate inventory can lead to a restaurant running out of an item on the menu. To avoid these situations, warehouse operators must put together the right orders, and drivers have to promptly deliver them. All the interactions customers have with employees must be positive and friendly. In summary, SYSCO has to deliver the right products, in the right condition, at the right time, and in a friendly manner.

Monitoring customer satisfaction is key to delivering services expertly and reliably. Knowing about your customer's valued outcomes is not enough. It is necessary to know the extent to which you are delivering those outcomes. SYSCO conducts frequent focus groups and customer satisfaction surveys (Appendix A) to determine whether the organization is or is not delivering valued customer outcomes.

As shown in Figure 3-4, SYSCO also has established frequent business reviews as part of its structure for prospecting, developing, and satisfying the most profitable customers. However, for such a structure to work effectively, a company must have high retention rates so its committed and loyal associates can find the opportunity areas to help each customer be more successful. This comprehensive approach focuses on the key customers and key potential customers and then identifies new sales opportunities, challenges to retention, and opportunities for greater account penetration. By better understanding each of its customer types' needs, the company has been able to develop new customer relationships and leverage current customer relationships.

Figure 3-4. Focusing on Satisfying Key Customers, SYSCO's Model

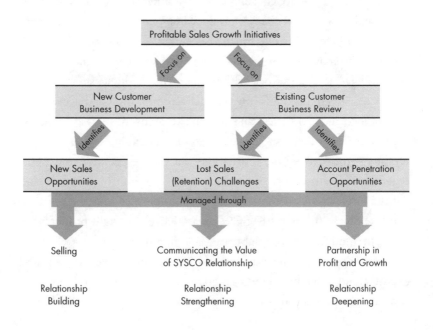

Building Profit through Building People

Overview

Going back to our basic model of the VPC, it is clear that a talented and satisfied employee base is critical to achieve and sustain customer satisfaction and loyalty. Even though customer retention seems like simple proposition, figuring out what your customers want and then delivering it can be extremely difficult. Effective execution requires knowing your customers and structuring your operations to align your employees' goals with your customers' needs. This requires making the conceptual and operational link between your employees and your customers.

The next chapter examines the importance of building employee loyalty and brand as a means of delivering value to your customers. Then, subsequent chapters walk you through the entire VPC and explain how to execute it effectively.

RECAP:

1. Profitability depends on the lifetime value of a customer thus making customer retention key.
2. Customer satisfaction and customer retention are accurate predictors of a firm's profitability.
3. Distinguish who your really good customers are. The top 10% can generate as much as 30–50% of the firm's profits.
4. To improve your profits:
   Identify your most profitable customers.
   Determine what those customers need.
   Deliver those services reliably.
   Monitor your service outcomes.
5. Having a satisfied workforce is key to provide the service required to keep the really good customers.

CHAPTER 4

Employee Loyalty and Satisfaction, and the Employer Brand

In the modern service economy, customer satisfaction is a central factor for organizational success. As discussed in Chapter 3, satisfying your most important customers requires knowing who they are and what they want, and then ensuring that they get it. Certainly most corporate offices have extensive data relevant to these questions, but some of the most important knowledge about customers resides within those who serve them: the employees. This is true in any business of any size in any industry.

Leveraging the power of employees requires examining the employment relationship from two sides. First, it is necessary to understand that the choices employees make have important consequences for the organization because they are in a position to provide a competitive advantage in the customer market. Second, we must understand how the organization's reputation (or in particular, its employer brand) can affect its performance in another important arena: the labor market.

The Importance of Employee Loyalty and Satisfaction

Employees are the critical interface between the organization and the customer. All the corporate customer research data in the world have no value unless employees have the skills, knowledge, motivation, and opportunity to deliver value to the customer. Employee loyalty and satisfaction are the starting points for customer satisfaction. Why are loyalty and satisfaction important? To understand why, we need to step back and understand the basic theory of work motivation. Building an organization where people are the source of competitive advantage requires recognition of two important aspects of employee motivation.

Understanding Employee Motivation

First, motivation is about far more than money. Economists, with their view of "rational economic man," tend to focus on monetary compensation as the major employee motivator. Although people possess rationality, they also possess heart and emotion. Economic outcomes are certainly an important factor in decision-making, but people also have social and moral considerations. Leveraging people necessitates attending to more than just the economic motivation of employees.

Consider the contrast between mercenaries and missionaries. Mercenaries epitomize the rational economic man. These are individuals whose skills, effort, and loyalties are available to the highest bidder. Certainly such individuals exist in the workplace, but too often employers assume that all employees are mercenaries who will work for anyone so long as the price is right. The result is that people begin to act like mercenaries.

In the early 1990's we heard much about the "new deal" and the "new employment relationship." Firms no longer promised employment, but employability. They continually bombarded employees with communications about how they had to take control of their own careers and become free agents. It is extremely difficult to build an organization's competitive advantage around such individuals, as was painfully illustrated later in the decade when the "war for talent" ensued. People who had been told to act like free agents—mercenaries—finally had opportunities to do so, and the turnover rate was disastrous for many companies.

In contrast, consider missionaries. Missionaries go almost anywhere in the world, even to the most uncomfortable and undeveloped places. They often perform menial tasks under daunting conditions. They usually work for a fraction of the wages they could make in other professions and often must conduct their own fundraising. Why? They do all this for a cause they believe in. Such individuals exemplify the social and moral dimensions of humankind. It is this mindset that Drucker (2003) referred to when he said "People do not work for an organization; they work for a cause." We will return to this concept later when we discuss the difference between being an employer of choice and having an employer brand.

Second, motivation is not about effort; it is about direction. Historically, people have focused on employee motivation as a question of effort. This perspective leads managers to ask the question, "How can I get my employees to increase their effort?" with the assumption that motivating employees requires getting them to be more energetic. This is a daunting task, given that "energy level" is substantially a function of nutrition, sleep, and overall health. Short of hiring nutritionists, sleep specialists, and personal trainers for each employee, there is little a manager can do to increase energy.

A more practical way to approach the motivational question is to recognize that managers have little control over their employees' energy level, but they can have a tremendous influence on energy *direction*, or the activities in which employees engage. This assumes that the employment relationship consists of a series of choices that employees make; consequently, the challenge for managers is to find ways to help employees make the choices that maximize benefit to the organization.

Attracting and Retaining the Right Employees

From this perspective, the importance of loyalty becomes obvious as it drives three general choices that can make or break your organization: the choice to join the firm, the choice to show up at work, and the choice to contribute.

Think back over your work history. Why did you choose the particular organizations you have joined? On the morning of your first day of work, how did you feel? Why did you feel this way? When you left an organization, why did you leave? And consider the worst firm competing in your industry. If that firm offered you a 10% pay increase over your present salary, would you go? How about 20%? How much of a pay increase would they have to offer you to get you to work for them? Why?

In today's labor market, the ability to attract and retain top employees directly influences organizational success. Many firms seem to narrowly define talent as the current and future leaders (both management and technological) of the organization, and they direct vast sums of money to staffing programs aimed at their attraction and retention. Certainly SYSCO cares about its top leaders, but unlike many other organizations, it focuses energy on *all* the talent in the company, particularly the people who serve customers.

Over the years, irrefutable data at SYSCO have shown that the longer the tenure of a marketing associate, the larger the sales volume he or she generates. Thus, every time the company loses a marketing associate, it is likely to lose sales revenues almost immediately. In addition, there are new costs in recruiting, training, and waiting for the learning curve of the replacement to catch up to the previous sales level. The loss of other "non-leader" critical employees has just as immediate an effect. Experienced warehouse staffers are far more productive and perform at higher quality (with fewer mistakes) than inexperienced ones. Experienced drivers, similarly, are more productive in their deliveries, have better knowledge about how to professionally and courteously interact with their customers, and know how to escape traffic jams. In addition, experienced drivers often have access to relevant knowledge of customers that they pass on to the marketing associates.

Turnover is costly in obvious ways: The cost of recruiting, hiring, and training each new employee can easily total several thousand dollars. Turnover also leads to less obvious costs that are revealed when you follow the links of the value-profit chain. Because customer satisfaction is the result of efforts by satisfied, capable employees, high turnover can reduce customer satisfaction in the following ways:

1. It creates less satisfied employees. An employee cannot thrive in a situation where his or her co-workers are constantly changing and where productivity is low.
2. New employees are less skilled at value creation. Even the most basic job has a learning curve. New employees must focus all of their attention on fundamental job responsibilities and have little time to deliver innovative solutions to customers.
3. Customers want to work with employees who not only understand their own jobs, but also understand how to apply that knowledge to make their customers' businesses more successful. This expertise only comes with time, continued development of employees, and true engagement in the business.
4. As employee retention and tenure grow, a business can move beyond fundamental excellence in execution and into a more profitable position through innovative approaches that create differentiation and true branding in the marketplace.

This line of thought is not simply anecdotal or based on our intuition. Table 4-1 demonstrates how much money a SYSCO business

Table 4-1. Improved Retention Equals Significant Savings, SYSCO

Position	Turnover Cost	2000 Retention Rate	2004 Retention Rate	Individual Business Unit Savings*	Corporation-wide Savings†
Marketing Associate	$50,000	75%	85%	$500,000	$50 million
Driver	$35,000	65%	80%	$525,000	$52.5 million
Night Warehouse Worker	$8,000	20%	50%	$240,000	$24 million
Total	–	–	–	$1.265 million	$126.5 million

*Assumes 100 Employees
†Assumes 10,000 Employees

unit can save by cutting its turnover in each of several job categories and how much the corporation can save.

Satisfied Employees Come to Work

Recall the words of Continental's Gordon Bethune: "I've never seen a successful company where people didn't want to come to work each day." Every organization faces the challenge of maintaining business processes in the face of some level of absenteeism. It may be necessary to hire temporary workers, shift some employees to other areas, or ask current employees to take on the increased workload. These stop-gap solutions are necessary; however, every one leads to less positive consequences than if no one had been absent. Firms often see a correlation between increased absenteeism and lower productivity, lower quality, and missed service opportunities."

At Continental Airlines, absenteeism had become such a hindrance that the company designed an incentive system to reward and recognize employees with perfect attendance. Each quarter Continental took from among the seven major job groups the names of all employ-

Building Profit through Building People

ees who had perfect attendance and entered them into a drawing. For each job group, one lucky individual was awarded a brand-new Ford Explorer painted in Continental's colors. Although the cost of the program was approximately $200,000 per quarter, the direct cost savings *far* exceeded that amount. In addition, there was an indirect positive effect from having trained, experienced, and committed employees in the workplace instead of untrained and inexperienced temporary help.

From the employee's perspective, the employment relationship is a series of choices. The choice to join a company is an important one, but it is not the only one. Once someone chooses to join, he or she faces a constant series of choices that aggregate over time. Across all employees, in every part of the company, these choices determine the company's success or failure. Each work day, employees wake up, a bit groggy, maybe slightly under the weather, or maybe with other pressures (from family) or opportunities (leisure) for how they will spend the next eight to ten hours. A company cannot succeed with customers unless it succeeds in getting employees to choose to come to work. Incentive programs do decrease absenteeism, but the more important efforts are on building an overall workplace where employees want to be, regardless of their chances of winning an incentive lottery.

Satisfied Employees Choose to Contribute to Success

Having once chosen to join a company and daily choosing to show up at work, employees face minute-by-minute choices about how they will spend their time and effort. This is the question of how they will behave at work, and this behavior is the key to an organization's success.

Industrial psychologists and human resource researchers suggest that employees engage in three types of behavior. First, *job behavior* entails all the things that employees are specifically asked to do as part of their jobs. For example, job descriptions identify the major areas of responsibility and the most frequently occurring or most important tasks. Second, *counterproductive behavior* consists of things that employees are explicitly or implicitly asked not to do, for example, product or material theft, time theft (taking extended breaks, surfing the Web), sabotage, and a host of other behaviors that have a direct negative impact. Finally, *discretionary behavior* describes opportunities for employees to make choices outside of their prescribed job tasks that have the potential to play a profound role in the organization's success. Discretionary behavior occurs when employees go above and beyond the call of duty, beyond their job descriptions, to make sure that a customer is served. It may mean helping someone from a different department even though there would be no payoff to the individual, or it may mean doing something for a customer that cements that customer's loyalty to the firm.

People become a source of competitive advantage when these three types of behavior occur in the right proportion. When employees engage in counterproductive behavior, a firm's performance cannot meet that of its competitors. When employees engage only in job-related behavior, the firm can meet but probably not exceed the performance of its competitors. But, when employees engage in discretionary behavior, they enable a firm to outperform competitors every time. Whether it is a Nordstrom sales associate changing the flat tire on a customer's car or a Southwest Airlines employee taking care of a customer's pet, when employees choose to serve customers beyond their job duties, their employers crush the competition.

The importance of discretionary behavior reinforces our earlier point that motivation is about more than just money. Because such behavior cannot reliably be predicted in advance, management cannot set up incentives guaranteed to drive it. Most often employees go beyond the call of duty because of their loyalty and commitment to the firm and their intrinsic desire to see it succeed. It is this emotional connection to the employer that distinguishes companies that build competitive advantage through people.

Where does this emotional connection come from? First, it distinguishes simply an "employer of choice" from a firm that has truly developed its own employer brand. Second, such an employer brand is built upon a set of management practices that create and reinforce the culture that treats people as the most important asset and consequently builds distinctiveness around this asset.

Building an Employer Brand

It is a common myth that efforts to enhance employee satisfaction should start with current employees. Satisfaction takes root much before that: The effort starts during recruiting. A company should aim to attract employees with the right fit, who really want to be with the company, find the work exciting, and come in with the confident attitude that they will enjoy their work.

The goal of many companies is to attract talent by being an "employer of choice." Employers of choice do not have to look for talented people. Talented people tend to find them and, more important, tend to stay with them. However, to most effectively leverage the value-profit chain, employers need to go beyond being employers of choice all the way to building an employer brand. Employer branding describes the unique relationship employees can have with a company. It is also useful in personifying the company's values and goals within its people.

Too often, an organization's efforts to be an employer of choice are mired in assumptions more consistent with the rational economic view of man. Firms seek to identify the critical factors of exchange such as compensation, pensions, health insurance, vacation days, development opportunities, and even a variety of nontraditional benefits such as concierge services, on-site gyms, and so forth. Such companies assume that if they offer the best total economic exchange, they will be able to attract and retain the right talent. Focusing exclusively on the economic exchange, however, is doomed to failure. Any aspect of monetary compensation can be met or exceeded by competitors, so becoming an employer of choice through economic exchange tactics only places a firm in an upward spiral of costs.

Developing an employer brand focuses on the larger values of the firm and leverages those values to create competitive advantage. Although it does not ignore the economic dimension, it goes beyond the rational economic man and builds also upon the social, moral, or self-actualizing dimensions of employees.

To make the distinction between an employer of choice and employer brand, consider SAS Institute and Microsoft. Both of these firms are in the software industry and have applicant pools that far exceed their hiring needs, enabling them to be quite selective about whom they hire. They both consistently make the list of *Fortune's* "100 Best Companies to Work For."

However, how many job-seekers would apply to *both* companies? Not many—because each company has such a distinctive employer brand. Words describing what it's like at SAS Institute include: freedom, teamwork, leisure, family time. These all make sense given SAS Institute's paternalistic culture that provides on-site schools, day care, and medical facilities and that discourages employees from working more than 35 hours a week. On the other hand, the following descriptors apply to Microsoft: wealth, innovative, aggressive, long hours, no personal life. These all make sense because Microsoft has an aggressive growth culture, built around doing whatever it takes to succeed (particularly in terms of spending many waking hours at work) but with the possibility of retiring very early and very rich. How many happy SAS employees do you think would be satisfied at Microsoft and vice versa? Note that both of these companies not only attract a large pool of applicants, but also they attract the *kinds* of applicants who will fit in their respective cultures. Being an employer of choice attracts applicants because of the package of total remuneration. Having an employer brand attracts applicants because of the values that are congruent between the employee and employer. Being an employer of choice attracts applicants. Having an employer brand attracts applicants who will fit.

The stronger the employer brand loyalty, the greater the pride and connection an employee feels toward the organization. A culture that fosters growth and innovation, employs effective leaders, and has a good product is more likely to evoke total employer brand commitment.

Employer branding is especially important in a tight labor market. When people are looking for a company to work for, they tend to lean toward those that have solid reputations and strong presences in their markets. If a company builds a strong internal employer brand and does a great job of publicizing that brand, all employees know what the company stands for and where it is going. Employees, in turn, communicate the brand to others. The result is that the corporate identity is very prevalent, making the company more attractive to job seekers who fit well in that environment, as well as to current employees.

Values, Brand, and Culture

The concept of organizational values has been much discussed within the management literature, and a plethora of value statements has been developed over the years. Nevertheless, declaring values is not the same as living out values in an organization. Many efforts to develop value statements have failed because these statements have been developed by top leaders who present their idealistic views of the organization absent any real knowledge of day-to-day activities. They seem to think that organizational values are like magic pixie dust; if they simply declare a set of values, then these values will suddenly appear and become deeply embedded in every employee.

Values develop over time, through deeply held beliefs constantly reinforced by communications, decisions, and processes. They do not appear by declaration, but rather by dedication, through managers who deeply believe in their efficacy and who are committed to living them every day.

Jim Collins in his book *Good to Great* (2001) noted that a firm's core values describe the basic principles to which the firm would adhere even if the business environment changed and the value no longer had efficacy for the firm's performance (Collins, 2001). O'Reilly and Pfeffer (2000) take a slightly different tack, arguing that most successful organizations have values that actually drive how the firm competes.

Organizational values consist of core values and secondary values. Another mistake top managers make in developing values statements is to create a laundry list of good things such as integrity, teamwork, and so forth, which, although desirable, cannot all possibly guide decision-making. The more values that are espoused, the more opportunities arise for conflicts among values. For example, what happens when acting with integrity goes against building team cohesiveness?

As a strong example of values, consider Seibel Systems, which specializes in developing and implementing customer relationship management software. Dissatisfied with his previous work experience at Oracle, Tom Seibel wanted to ensure that the culture at the company he founded and that bears his name would have customer satisfaction deeply ingrained within it. He sought to build a culture fundamentally the opposite of what he called the "pathological Silicon Valley corporate culture." Seibel Systems' core values of customer satisfaction, professional courtesy, professionalism, and goal and action orientation, have provided a clear basis for guiding organizational decision-making. (Chang & O'Reilly, 2001).

Similarly, SYSCO embraces only three underlying core values or principles for business management. First, *entrepreneurial* is the company's way of promoting a mindset among its business leaders, who exercise discretion on how they run their local businesses. The role of the corporate office is to ensure that businesses are achieving desired results in terms of revenues, profits, and so on. When a business struggles, the corporate office intervenes by providing ideas, services, or other support. But a driving principle is to do everything possible to leverage necessary economies of scale and to make business leaders feel and act like entrepreneurs in their local markets.

Second, *high-quality service* is the key by which SYSCO differentiates itself from competitors. The company prides itself on operating efficiently and on providing innovative products and services to meet customers' needs through business processes that deliver the right product, to the right place, at the right time. The goal is to do everything possible to make customers successful, and that principle has to be embraced by every individual in every position, regardless of whether they have direct contact with customers.

The third key value that is critical and possibly the most important to SYSCO's ongoing success is *integrity*—in every sense of the word. Integrity means the financial integrity of operating the business, as well as the value of integrity exercised by treating all stakeholders with dignity and respect and consistently meeting or exceeding expectations.

Tying Employer Brand to Customer Experience

Remember that the employer brand aims to attract and retain the right kind of people, those who fit with your culture and strategy. It's also important to note that most successful firms have cultures and strategies that are difficult to separate. For example, it would be virtually impossible to effectively implement a strategy of customer service without having built a culture of customer service. Similarly, an orientation toward customer service must be an integral part of the employer brand to support the culture that supports the strategy.

Consider Southwest Airlines' recent campaign advertising "Freedom" ("You are now free to move about the country."). This effort communicates to customers that Southwest provides a freedom for travel (low prices, little need for advanced purchases, a large number of cities served, etc.). Interestingly, Southwest communicates a similar message to its employees. The internal company Web site is structured around different "freedoms" for employees (e.g., "Free to choose benefits"). This example shows how the employer brand can communicate the same employee experience as customer experience.

For an even more specific example, let's examine SYSCO's concept of the entrepreneurial mindset. Remember that many of the company's best customers are entrepreneurs—small business restaurants that are family owned and operated. Even large-chain customers are often built on a franchise model within which franchisees are running their own businesses. These people value the opportunity to run their own businesses. So when they work with SYSCO a kinship exists because they are essentially a local small business doing business with another local small business. The entrepreneurial aspect creates symmetry between the company and our customers.

Going to the next level, SYSCO tries as much as possible to build the entrepreneurial approach into its employer brand. Marketing associates, like most outside salespeople, view themselves as entrepreneurial consultants. They are provided with the best in tools, training, technology, and products, but they have the freedom to serve their local customers as those customers need.

But what about other jobs, for instance, the delivery driver? In just about every customer service business these people are paid on an hourly basis. They are given a route to run, 8 hours to complete it, and are encouraged to be only productive enough to not go over the time allotted. Over the past few years, however, some SYSCO drivers have been offered activity-based compensation. In this approach, drivers are paid for the work they do, not for the time they spend. These drivers can manage their own time to finish early if they want. Consequently, the company creates entrepreneurial drivers, working in an entrepreneurial culture, with entrepreneurial customers.

Overview

Achieving success is all about people and understanding that link in the value-profit chain. Success in the marketplace comes when employees have the skills, motivation, and opportunity to engage in behavior that provides superior products and services. Building success through people, then, requires that firms are successful in the labor market at attracting and retaining people with the right skills as well as values that fit with those of the organization.

In the next chapter, we will describe the 5-STAR model for creating competitive advantage through employees.

RECAP:

1. Building employee loyalty and satisfaction is critical to a firm's success because:

    Loyal employees are more motivated.

    Loyalty attracts and retains employees.

    Satisfied employees choose to come to work.

    Satisfied employees choose to contribute to firm success.

2. Creating a work environment where employees want to go beyond their job requirements to serve customers can distinguish your organization from its competitors.

3. Building an employer brand attracts and retains the right kind of people to fit your organization's culture and strategy and aligns your employees' work experience with your customers' valued outcomes.

CHAPTER 5

The 5-STAR Model Employer Brand

In the previous chapter, we examined the importance of people when it comes to competitive advantage in the customer market, and we looked at the critical need to build an employer brand in the labor market. Building an employer brand requires identifying the core values of the organization and building a management model that continually communicates and reinforces those values. Here we will describe the values of a basic 5-STAR management model similar to the one developed by and used at Continental and SYSCO. In the subsequent chapter, we will provide a more detailed description of the kinds of practices that exemplify these values and a management model that makes those values apparent to employees.

The 5-STAR Framework

The STAR model attracts, supports, and retains top talent for long tenure by encouraging employees to choose to come to work and to contribute to the organization's success. Creating a STAR organization provides a strong link from employees to customer needs to profitable growth. The STAR stands for the five-dimension framework that the company executes. The basic framework is depicted in Figure 5-1. The point system, from a low of 0.00 to 5.00 at the highest, is based on the satisfaction level scores from the work-climate survey.

A company at the 1-STAR level is one that is not engaging its people at any level other than a pure transactional exchange. The environment has not elicited commitment to the job, the company, or the corporation. Employees are prone to leave the organization for just about any reason, but really their departure may not be a loss. The organization, however, cannot maintain any ability to attract and retain talent.

A company at the 2-STAR level has created an environment where employees at least engage emotionally in their own jobs. They take pride in what they do but not necessarily in the company for

Figure 5-1. The 5-STAR Model

★★★★★	★★★★	★★★	★★	★
4.00–5.00	3.90–4.00	3.75–3.89	3.55–3.74	< 3.54
Total Brand Commitment	**Brand Culture**	**Employer Brand**	**Job Brand**	**Job**
Provides optimal work experience and self-worth. Employer brand is synonymous with business and individual success.	Sum of corporate attributes is greater than the parts. The company embodies what the employee's work function is.	Employee sees self as part of the company.	Employee sees some emotional value in the job and takes pride in doing the job.	Employee sees only the job (e.g., type of work, pay, hours).

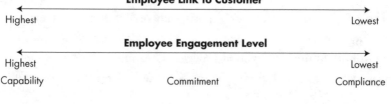

Employee Link to Customer

Highest   Lowest

Employee Engagement Level

Highest   Lowest

Capability   Commitment   Compliance

which they do it. A 2-STAR organization can execute basic processes at a level that may match competitors but probably is at a bit of a
disadvantage and is certainly not positioned for long-term growth.

A company at the 3-STAR level emotionally engages employees in
their jobs and begins to engage them in the company. The employees, while maybe not completely identifying with the company, at
least feel that they are part of the company rather than simply free
agents doing their jobs. This type of organization can probably match
the performance of its competitors but is unlikely to surpass them.

A company at the 4-STAR level is one that can deliver superior
service and performance relative to its competitors. It has built a culture that engages people in their jobs and in the company—at all levels from departmental, to divisional, to corporate. In SYSCO, for
example, employees recognize that the brand has been built nationally as numerous autonomous companies have adhered to a common
set of values.

Finally, a company that excels at implementing this framework
rates as a 5-STAR company, one that has built a truly effective
employer brand. Employees are deeply engaged in their jobs, their
organization, and the larger corporation. They derive personal satisfaction from being part of the company brand and recognize that it
is synonymous with business and individual success. These companies consistently outperform their competitors, and the culture creates an advantage that endures in the long run. Consistent with the
value-profit chain, these employers enjoy higher return on investment, greater customer satisfaction, and lower turnover rates than
their competitors.

But what really constitutes a STAR model—the basic management model that describes how a company seeks to engage the hearts
and minds of employees with its employer brand? And what dimensions, or principles, do you use to build one?

5-STAR Dimensions

At Continental and SYSCO—and at any company that uses the value-profit chain—the STAR model is all about taking care of people. The model gives the same respect to employees as it does to customers. In fact, STAR model companies have two types of customers:

1. Those employed by the company: Treat them fairly, pay them well, and they will treat the end customer well.
2. The end customers, who are whomever you have to treat well.

You can implement the STAR framework no matter what type of company structure or business model you have. At SYSCO, for example, implementation was different than at Continental—and than it would be at many organizations. Because SYSCO comprises many autonomous businesses, it does not use directives that force those businesses to do certain things. So it was necessary to find a way to create agreement around basic ideas without requiring uniformity in practice. Consequently, a set of 5-STAR dimensions, or principles, allow businesses wide discretion in actual implementation. These principles are:

1. Ensuring that leaders offer direction and support.
2. Strengthening front-line supervisors.
3. Rewarding performance.
4. Including employees by engaging them and leveraging diversity.
5. Addressing employees' quality of life.

If effectively executed, these principles comprise a STAR brand through which people feel strongly committed to the company and thus deliver superior performance to customers. The following sections are an overview of these 5-STAR dimensions. More detail is provided in the next chapter regarding how these actually get implemented in an intervention framework. Here we present them and provide examples of the variety of management practices that have been used to implement them in different business units.

Leadership Direction and Support

The best performance thrives under facilitative leadership in which the leaders of the company and its employees have a personal connection to the goals of the company and to each other. Leadership direction and support is:

1. First providing the vision, mission, and goal-setting framework.
2. Then creating the work environment for executing the organization's mission and goals through constant and consistent communication with the rank and file about the direction of the business and about their concerns.

Strengthening Front-Line Supervisors

Supervisors are among the most critical and ignored elements in building an employer brand. In too many companies top leaders are considered to be the only critical human capital. There is an assumption that these individuals define direction and strategy—and that once those are defined, everything else will hum like a well-oiled machine. Organizations, though, are not machines. They are collections of human beings whose interactions with one another can critically determine whether strategy will be effectively or ineffectively executed.

Because supervisors are on the front lines, they make or break the day-to-day execution of your company's critical goals. To the employee, the front-line supervisor *is* the company. How employees are treated by their supervisors vastly influences the employees' beliefs about and attitudes toward the company. It is in the organization's best interest to make sure that supervisors have the skills to excel at delivering desired results and that they are equipped to help the people they supervise develop their own essential skills.

Rewards for Performance

What distinguishes entrepreneurs from managers? Certainly entrepreneurs tend to be more innovative, but, more importantly, their rewards are more closely tied to performance. If they have great ideas and execute them well, they can succeed financially. If they have bad ideas or do not execute well, they will fail miserably and not reap financial rewards. All employees need to have a strong tie between their performances and their rewards.

Although rewarding performance sounds easy, doing so effectively often requires rethinking the traditional view of rewards. Certainly money motivates, but employees are social, as well as economic, beings and they have families, colleagues, and others who help them to define their success—professionally and personally. Thus, rewarding performance also can consist of finding opportunities to let those closest to employees (usually spouses or parents) not only know of the company's appreciation for their hard work, but also to participate in the recognition.

Inclusion through Engagement and Diversity

Inclusion encompasses a whole host of activities. The word "inclusion" describes the basic principle that all employees are part of the company and therefore need to be included in many, if not all, aspects of the business. This means that employees need to have access to information about business performance, the challenges and issues that the company faces, and the goals it seeks to achieve. It also means that they are included in decisions, particularly those that affect their specific work environment. Finally, it means that they are included regardless of their race, sex, job function and even, to some extent, their level in the hierarchy.

Employees who know how their performances measure up and how they contribute to the company's success have the information they need to feel pride in their accomplishments—and to improve their performances. Today's leaders encourage and coach their people to learn continuously—not just to meet the requirements of their current jobs but to go beyond in preparation for advancement. An employee's ability to see the connection between his or her work and the company's strategic objectives drives positive behavior. In addition, there must be a focus on creating a diverse workforce that values and leverages differences among people, cultures, and capabilities.

Quality of Life

One inarguable lesson from the war-for-talent era was that although employees want to develop, grow, and be rewarded for their work, they also want to find ways to balance their work and personal lives. Obviously, different individuals have different ideas of what constitutes balance between work and family, but too few companies recognize these individual differences. Companies often institute one-size-fits-all approaches, usually based on the assumptions of the top leaders about what constitutes work/life balance.

Increasingly, people are seeking to find better balance between their work with their personal lives and families. A strategic work/life approach can mesh these two sides of people's lives, meeting the needs of the business and the needs of its employees. Some examples of systematic changes—not just add-on programs—that have helped employees achieve this challenging goal include:

- flex time (e.g., staggered start times and 9-day/80-hour pay periods)
- discounts on child care/elder care

- referrals through a buying service for everything from car repair to veterinarians
- floating holidays that let employees choose when to be off
- telecommuting
- supervisors who have learned to coach better to create a less stressful work environment

5-STAR Model Goal—A Winning Culture

Just as customers make the final decisions about the usefulness of your company's products and services, the employees determine whether you have developed an employer brand. The goal of the 5-STAR model is to create a culture that sends a clear message that people are valued; in fact, they are just as important as customer satisfaction and stock price. One basic concept in marketing is that price will be the driver if all else is equal and there is no brand loyalty. With its customers and employees, a company can work to build its brand, and thus loyalty, by offering services that are not easily replicated by competitors. Even if a competitor offers a higher salary to an associate or lower price to a customer, these people will not leave because they value the overall relationship and value-added services.

Are Five Stars Enough?

So far you may see nothing wrong with the 5-STAR model and believe that all these dimensions seem to make great sense. However, a reasonable question comes to mind: Why five? Certainly a number of other dimensions exist that might help to create a winning culture and employer brand in your own company. We suggest that you think about how many dimensions would best describe how to build your winning culture. We settled on five principles or dimensions for three basic reasons.

First, research by the Corporate Leadership Council in 2002 looked at the effectiveness of different interventions for boosting employee performance (Corporate Leadership Council, 2002). The Council examined 106 different performance-management drivers and levers and found that:

- The most effective performance management strategy is composed of a portfolio of carefully selected organizational, managerial, and employee-related levers.
- The effectiveness of performance management levers varies tremendously, improving or destroying performance by up to 40%. Levers must be chosen and prioritized with precision.

Most of the interventions involved leadership support, front-line supervisor coaching and feedback, face-to-face communication with employees, and reward systems. Sound familiar? They should because they are very similar to four of the STAR guiding principles.

Second, two of the dimensions are included simply because we feel strongly about employers being socially responsible. We truly believe that leveraging diversity and attending to employees' work-life balance helps attract, motivate, and retain a highly talented workforce. The added bonus is that these dimensions enhance corporate performance.

Third, although an endless number of dimensions might exist, our experience is that human nature dictates a reasonably small number of dimensions in order to maintain focus. Learning theories teach that short-term memory can only hold "the magic number seven, plus or minus two." This means that people can usually only hold between five and nine pieces of information in their short-term memory. To drive a mental management model into the thoughts and behaviors of managers and supervisors (whether they number in the tens or the thousands), we believe that a simpler, more concise model works best.

Overview

This 5-STAR model has served SYSCO and Continental well, as later chapters will show. We have described here the basic skeleton of the model. In the next few chapters we will show you how it was implemented and provide you with ideas and tools for how you might implement the model in your own organization.

RECAP:

1. Building a 5-STAR employer brand requires identifying the main levers that have an impact on your employees.
2. The 5-STAR model focuses on:
   - Ensuring that leaders offer direction and support, particularly to front-line employees.
   - Strengthening front-line supervisors because they have the greatest impact on front-line employees.
   - Rewarding performance at all levels and in creative ways.
   - Including employees by engaging them and leveraging diversity.
   - Addressing employees' quality of life.

CHAPTER 6

The 5-STAR Management Model

The previous chapter described the basics behind creating a 5-STAR model to build an employer brand. That chapter described the drivers of the STAR model as well as some practices that support those drivers. In this chapter, we will lay out a process as well as a set of tools and some examples to show how to build a 5-STAR management model. While you may not want to imitate the examples from Continental and SYSCO exactly, they will provide ideas that enable your organization to move from its present state toward achieving its goal of being a 5-STAR employer.

Building a STAR management model entails five basic steps:

1. *Strategic planning:* Revise and integrate critical strategic planks for sustained profitability.
2. *Goal setting:* Set companywide goals.
3. *Assessing the current state:* Determine what current performance levels are and measure progress along each driver.
4. *Interpreting and prioritizing:* Identify the key drivers that need improvement in the short term.
5. *Implementing programs for improvement:* Identify and develop programs that effectively exhibit a 5-STAR management model.

Strategic Planning

Many organizations have a strategic planning process, and these systems are as individual as the companies. But strategic planning often does not translate into goals in the workplace. One key to successful strategic planning is a well-integrated, dynamic strategic process that is supported by everyone in the management chain. The process should be reviewed regularly with senior management and discussed with the board of directors. Senior management not only should ensure that the strategy is communicated throughout the organization, but also should link the goal-setting process and operational initiatives to each of the planks in the strategic plan.

Goal Setting

SYSCO uses a Balanced Scorecard approach, developed by Kaplan and Norton (1996), as one of the management tools for planning and monitoring the corporation's performance as well as each individual company's performance. The goals are divided into four basic performance areas:

- financial
- customer
- operational
- human capital.

Prior to the start of each fiscal year, each company's leadership team sets two to three goals in each of the four basic areas. These goals are then cascaded and modified throughout that particular operating company.

The balanced scorecard begins with financial results because that is the measure that shareholders and analysts tend to put the greatest weight on. It describes the aspects of financial performance that the company will use to assess its success.

The scorecard's second aspect delineates how customers affect financial results. The customer area contains the measures relevant to customers that management believes are most critical to achieving financial performance goals.

The third, operational, area describes the aspects of day-to-day operational performance that are most relevant to achieving customer and financial goals.

Finally, the human capital component reflects management's beliefs about the aspects of the workforce that are relevant to satisfying customers and achieving financial results. The measures here consist of those that management believes most strongly drive customer and financial performance.

There are many exciting aspects of the balanced scorecard approach. First, it forces managers to sit down and explicitly articulate their theory of the business. Too often, decision-makers hold implicit theories that guide their decisions but fail to recognize internal contradictions to those theories. Second, it encourages the top management team to develop a shared or consensus theory that will enable them to make decisions with greater coordination and cooperation. Third, because the approach is based on objective measures, it allows top management to test the validity of their theories. This critical link will be explored in the next chapter.

One example of a balanced scorecard metrics report is presented in Figure 6-1. This chart shows the four major areas measured at SYSCO, as well as the major drivers for each area. Specific metrics are calculated for each company and then used to give an overall performance perspective and corporate ratings.

As you can see from the figure, the human capital component has a number of drivers. Associate satisfaction—as reported by the Climate Survey metric—is one of the central drivers: Not only does it have an impact on other aspects, but it also is strongly tied to superior operating

Figure 6-1. Balanced Scorecard Metrics, SYSCO

Customer Drivers
- Account Penetration
- Service Level
- Pieces per Error
- SYSCO Brand
- Clean Invoices
- Customer Climate

Human Capital Drivers
- Payroll per Piece
- Climate Survey
- Marketing Associate Retention
- Driver Retention
- Worker's Compensation as a % of Sales
- Employees per 100K Cases

Financial Drivers
- Sales Growth
- Margin
- Return on Capital
- Operating Expenses
- Operating Pretax Earnings
- Earnings Growth

Operational Drivers
- Delivery Expense
- Warehouse Expense
- Pieces per trip
- Inventory Shrink
- Cost per Case
- Cases per Man Hour

Sample Human Capital Metrics Report*

Company	Payroll per Piece		Climate Survey Score		Marketing Associate Retention		Driver Retention		Worker's Compensation, % of Sales		No. of Employees per 100K Cases		Overall Rank
	June 05	June 04	June 05	June 04	June 05	June 04	June 05	June 04	June 05	June 04	June 05	June 04	
Company A	$3.15	$3.17	3.89	3.89	82%	80%	83%	79%	9%	11%	4.33	4.38	38
Company B	$2.48	$2.50	3.93	3.88	88%	87%	89%	87%	2%	4%	3.80	3.89	5
Company C	$2.59	$2.63	3.80	3.75	84%	82%	84%	81%	9%	10%	3.90	4.10	25

* Numbers and percentages are representative, not actual. Comparisons and trends are accurate.

performance, as we will show later. To illustrate how the scorecard works, we will focus on the associate satisfaction component.

The ultimate goal—besides financial success—is to be a 5-STAR employer and a 5-STAR service provider. Achieving the former leads to the latter, hence the strong emphasis on associate satisfaction. As the 5-STAR model shows, every company should strive to create total brand commitment among its associates. This model provides a guiding framework for decision-making in regard to human capital and presents the challenging but achievable goal of becoming a 5-STAR company.

Assessing the Current State

Once the goals have been set, you must assess where your organization currently stands relative to those goals. Ongoing self-assessments are crucial in helping to establish and institutionalize cultures that focus on the connection between associates and customers and on a potential win-win relationship between them. The self-assessments also form a framework for building positive changes in the ongoing effort to delight associates, customers, and shareholders through continuous improvement and outstanding business results.

To determine associate satisfaction, each SYSCO operating company conducts a comprehensive, annual self-assessment as well as impromptu and informal assessments on an as-needed basis. The work-climate survey measures associate satisfaction levels and includes sections on each of the main drivers of associate satisfaction. This survey also enables companies to determine which drivers of satisfaction may be lacking. Appendix B is a sample cover letter from the CEO highlighting how the survey feedback is used, and Appendix C is the work-climate instrument. SYSCO has contracted with Cornell University to implement the survey and tabulate aggregate results. This "arms-length" approach encourages associates to be forthright in their responses because the individual completed surveys are never seen by executives at the sponsoring company.

The goals in terms of work climate at the operating companies are

- a satisfaction score of at least 4.0 out of a possible 5.0;
- sixty percent or more of associates describing themselves as satisfied or very satisfied; and
- continual improvement of associates' performance.

Five-STAR status is conferred on companies that score 4.0 or greater on an aggregate of the associate satisfaction measures. Some of the operating companies are closer than others to reaching a 5-STAR rating because very few organizations have *all five* of the STAR characteristics. Companies that have experienced significant growth but lack effective leadership practices will only go so far before their limitations hinder success. To truly achieve and sustain 5-STAR status, an organization must instill processes over time that focus on developing associate commitment. Again, because the work-climate survey also assesses the drivers of satisfaction, it can be a powerful tool for determining exactly where a company may be failing and consequently enable the company to more efficiently and effectively respond to customers' needs.

Interpreting and Prioritizing

After completing the survey once or twice, the management of each operating company gains an understanding of its current standing among associates and can thus determine reasonable action steps for achieving its goals. Progress is made in steps, not leaps. Operating companies are encouraged to identify areas of opportunity and to work from there.

In developing your own STAR system, how do you know which areas should receive greatest priority? Obviously, you might focus first on the dimensions that have the lowest overall scores. Although reasonable, such an approach is not always optimal. The most brightly burning fire may not necessarily be the most important one to put out first. In other words, it may not be immediately apparent which of the drivers should receive top priority. The first few years of the process of developing and implementing the work-climate survey should bring understanding of the most important drivers of organizational effectiveness.

At SYSCO, the integration of associate and customer satisfaction surveys has provided significant insights to the key practices that have the most impact. The dimension that proved to require the most attention is effective training of front-line supervisors. The work-climate survey has shown that it is the supervisors who have the largest and most direct impact on associate satisfaction. The dimensions that mirror the 5-STAR model are:

- Ensure that leaders offer direction and support.
- Strengthen your front-line supervisors.
- Rewards and recognition.
- Inclusion for engagement and diversity.
- Address your associates' quality of life.

As Figure 6-2 indicates, not all components of the STAR model are equal. Front-line supervisors, leadership support, and rewards have the greatest impact on associate satisfaction. This figure shows the allocation of time to each dimension. Keep in mind that different companies would set different priorities. Priorities for your company will depend on your people and business and be based on the first few assessments and correlations.

Managers at the SYSCO corporate office and operating companies receive their specific location's scores on the survey, accompanied by a

Figure 6-2. Prioritized Dimensions in the STAR Model, SYSCO

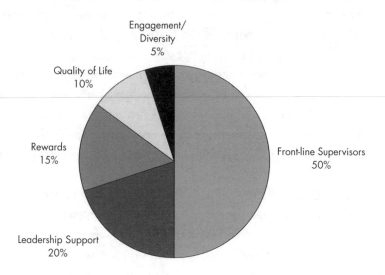

packet that explains how to interpret the results and includes a list of best practices to improve results in each area and some recommendations for action. The packet also has a progress worksheet to be used in the implementation phase, described below. In addition, the operating companies' presidents and HR managers receive customized charts and graphs that are tailored to their company's specific results. This presentation is provided as a guide to assist managers discussing the results with the appropriate departments (operations, marketing/sales, administration, and so on). The managers are encouraged to review their results and to develop action plans to improve areas of opportunity.

Leaders of operating companies then complete an action planning worksheet, identify areas of opportunity, and are directed to the section of their packets pertaining to recommended best practices. For each dimension on the survey (and of the STAR model), there is a list of programs and ideas that have proven successful at various operating companies. Figure 6-3 is a worksheet that correlates the items on the work-climate survey with various actions that could be taken to

Building Profit through Building People

Figure 6-3. Key Actions to Improve Results of Work Climate Survey, SYSCO*

The charts below list attributes of the work climate survey and different actions that you and your team can take to have an impact on each area. Depending on what elements you need to strengthen, you can find appropriate activities below. Remember to challenge your team to execute one idea well rather than executing many ideas ineffectively.

LEADERSHIP SUPPORT	Key Actions				
	1.	2.	3.	4.	5.
	Coaching & Maximizing Performance	President's Roundtable	Monthly Senior Management Meetings	Annual State of the Company Address	Executive Team Presence
A1. I know what is expected of me at work.	✓			✓	
A2. I have a reasonable workload to do my job well.	✓				
A3. At work, I have the opportunity to put my skills to good use.	✓				
A4. I have an opportunity to influence decisions that directly impact my work.		✓	✓		✓
A5. I am informed whenever decisions are to be made that affect my job.		✓		✓	
A6. I know the business goals of the company.	✓	✓	✓	✓	✓
A7. Communication from upper management (President, Executive Vice President, etc.) is open and honest.		✓	✓	✓	✓
A8. Upper management demonstrates their commitment to build a diverse workforce.		✓	✓	✓	✓
A9. Upper management (President, Executive Vice President, etc.) spends time talking with associates about our business direction.	✓	✓	✓	✓	

*NOTE: Section B of the survey is not part of this report to managers.

Figure 6-3, continued

STRENGTHEN FRONTLINE SUPERVISOR (FLS)	Key Actions					
	1. Strengthen FLS Program	2. Monthly Supervisory Meetings	3. Training Resources	4. Coaching & Maximizing Performance	5. Coaching	6. Feedback
B1. My supervisor treats me with dignity and respect.	✓		✓	✓	✓	✓
B2. My supervisor cares about me as a person.	✓			✓	✓	✓
B3. I receive timely, specific, fair, and ongoing feedback.	✓		✓	✓	✓	✓
B4. My supervisor encourages my involvement in solving a problem or improving a situation.	✓	✓	✓	✓	✓	
B5. My supervisor helps me whenever I ask for help.	✓			✓	✓	
B6. My supervisor and I review my top goals and discuss how they contribute to the company's success.	✓			✓	✓	✓
B7. When I make a mistake, my supervisor and I share ideas on what I could have done differently.	✓	✓		✓	✓	✓
B8. I have received constructive feedback on my performance within the last 6 months.	✓			✓	✓	✓
B9. My supervisor encourages my career development.	✓			✓	✓	✓
B10. My supervisor does his/her best to make SYSCO a good place to work.	✓	✓	✓	✓	✓	
B11. My supervisor is quite competent in doing his/her job.	✓	✓				
B12. My supervisor removes obstacles so I can do my job better.	✓	✓	✓	✓	✓	✓

Figure 6-3, continued

| | Key Actions | | | | | |
| | 1. | 2. | 3. | 4. | 5. | 6. |
QUALITY OF LIFE	SYSCOSafe	Ethics Hotline Meetings	All-Purpose Leave	SYSCO S.T.E.P.	One-on-One Meetings	Family Gatherings
C1. I trust what the company tells me.		✓			✓	
C2. I know whom to call to get help solving problems.	✓	✓			✓	
C3. I feel our rules and procedures do not prevent me from doing a good job.	✓				✓	
C4. Different departments of our company work together to get the job done.	✓					
C5. I have the proper materials and equipment I need to do my job right.	✓			✓		
C6. I feel my work environment is safe.	✓				✓	
C7. I like the people I work with.						✓
C8. This is a good place to work.	✓	✓	✓	✓		✓
C9. My co-workers and I take the initiative to solve workplace problems together.	✓				✓	
C10. I have received sufficient training to do my job effectively.	✓				✓	
C11. I have had opportunities to learn new things at work within the past year.				✓		
C12. I am given opportunities to learn and develop new skills for future advancement.				✓		
C13. Compared to other companies in my area, I feel SYSCO is accommodating to my work and family balance.			✓		✓	✓
C14. I feel SYSCO is generally responsive to my work and personal concerns.	✓	✓	✓	✓	✓	✓
C15. My organization values the contributions of employees regardless of race, gender, or ethnic background.		✓	✓	✓	✓	
C16. My organization has a culture that fosters new ideas from employees regardless of race, gender, or ethnic background.		✓	✓	✓		✓

Figure 6-3, continued

	Key Actions					
	1.	**2.**	**3.**	**4.**	**5.**	**6.**
REWARDS	ABC Comp (Delivery)	Competitive Wage Survey	Benefits Statements	Recognition & Service Awards	ABC Comp (Whse)	International Job Posting /S.T.E.P
E1. I feel I am being paid a fair amount for the work I do.	✓	✓	✓		✓	
E2. My pay is the same or better than that of other companies in our market.	✓	✓	✓		✓	
E3. My benefits are the same or better than those of other companies in our market.	✓	✓	✓		✓	
E4. Doing my job well leads to monetary rewards.	✓			✓	✓	
E5. Doing my job well leads to recognition and respect from those I work with.	✓			✓	✓	✓
E6. My supervisor seeks opportunities to provide me with positive feedback on a job well done.				✓		
E7. Decisions made about promotions or job changes within this organization are fair.				✓		✓

improve the score on that item. The worksheet is divided into sections based on the STAR dimensions.

Leaders of operating companies are encouraged to look over the suggested key actions and select a couple from each dimension where there is opportunity for improvement. It is not necessary for them to implement every program at once. Rather, they are asked to look at potential areas of opportunity and identify which best practices they could benefit from the most at this point. After they have successfully implemented one or two, they may return to the list and choose another.

Figure 6-3, continued

	Key Actions					
	1.	2.	3.	4.	5.	6.
INCLUSION FOR DIVERSITY/ENGAGEMENT	Orientation of New Associates	Employee Advocate Meetings	SYSCO S.T.E.P. Program	Employee Feedback	Targeted Selection & Recruitment	Community Involvement /Diversity
F1. I am willing to work harder to help this company succeed.	✓		✓			
F2. I am proud to work for SYSCO.	✓	✓	✓			✓
F3. I feel a strong sense of belonging to this organization.	✓	✓	✓	✓	✓	✓
F4. I feel a diverse workforce contributes to SYSCO's success.					✓	✓
F5. I am comfortable building relationships with peers or customers who are different from me.	✓			✓		✓
F6. I would refer a friend to come work at SYSCO.			✓		✓	✓
F7. I provide constructive suggestions about how my department can improve its effectiveness.	✓	✓	✓	✓	✓	

Implementing Programs for Improvement

Once the goals are set, the current state assessed, and the issues and challenges ranked according to priority, leaders and decision-makers need to develop programs to help move from the current state to the goal. Implementing the 5-STAR model requires developing new programs to support the model while also identifying and bolstering existing programs that already exemplify the employer brand.

A progress worksheet (Figure 6-4) also is normally included in the packet of survey results. The HR staff or the operating company's president is encouraged to review the company's results and then complete this worksheet. It is also recommended that a representative from each

Figure 6-4. STAR Progress Worksheet, SYSCO Operating Companies

Completed by: _____ Location: _____ Return Completed Worksheet to _____ by _____ (date)

STAR Principle	Range of Scores	SYSCO Goal	Your Local Score	Best Practices for Impact Select Two (2) Actions for Implementation	Implementation Date
Leadership Support		4.0		___ Implement president's round table ___ Conduct annual state of the company address ___ Conduct monthly senior management meetings; discuss supervisors' and employees' issues ___ Review and act on findings of the work climate survey and key actions ___ Other (please insert your best practice here): ___ Other (please insert your best practice here):	
Strengthening Frontline Supervisor		4.0		___ Conduct monthly supervisors' meeting to discuss HR metrics and how to effect change ___ Implement Strengthening the Frontline Supervisors leadership training program ___ Utilize the coaching worksheet ___ Align supervisor incentives with organization's human capital goals ___ Other (please insert your best practice here): ___ Other (please insert your best practice here):	
Quality of Life		4.0		___ Implement SYSCOSafe ___ Conduct one-on-one discussions ___ Implement ABC pay for drivers ___ Publicize the ethics hotline and suggestion opportunities ___ Other (please insert your best practice here): ___ Other (please insert your best practice here):	
Rewards		4.0		___ Implement ABC pay structure ___ Publish benefit statements ___ Conduct competitive wage survey ___ Special occasions for special rewards ___ Other (please insert your best practice here): ___ Other (please insert your best practice here):	
Inclusion for Diversity/ Engagement		4.0		___ Enhance employee orientation program ___ Conduct employee advocate meetings ___ Utilize targeted selection for hiring high-quality people ___ Implement SYSCOSafe ___ Other (please insert your best practice here): ___ Other (please insert your best practice here):	
Overall		4.0			

department within the company be included in a session where they can all collaborate on the worksheet.

Below are sections describing each STAR dimension. Each section explains how the STAR model works and has examples of actions taken to reach 5-STAR status. For some of these drivers, you will also see the worksheets that guide the operating companies in responding to survey results and in designing the appropriate actions. We have tried to provide as many of the tools as possible so that you will not need to start from scratch. These tools can also be found on the Web site of the Society for Human Resource Management (SHRM) at www.shrm.org/books/buildingprofit/tools.

1. Ensure that Your Leaders Offer Direction and Support

One of the most common reasons why implementation of the value-profit chain fails is lack of leadership commitment and support. Business competence and strategic capability are more highly developed in today's leaders than is their ability to connect personally with employees. Yet research shows that being trustworthy, showing empathy, and creating meaning are the characteristics that differentiate high-performing leaders from the rest. We've found that in vastly different companies and in both turnarounds and steadily performing companies, leaders are most effective if they integrate personal connection with business competence.

One of the foremost responsibilities of leaders is to establish and communicate a vision and mission that all employees understand and support. The model starts with critical leadership-support ideas and practices. Even though many employees do not know their executive leaders personally, involved leaders who can influence a group of people to achieve a common goal generate the greatest success for their organizations.

Every operating company kicks off its work-climate survey with a memorandum from the CEO to all employees to demonstrate the importance of their feedback and to highlight some changes that were implemented based on previous survey results (see Appendix B).

The importance of face-time with associates cannot be emphasized enough. A president from a successful operating company says it this way, "The price of admission to become a STAR employer is the dedication of top management to be involved with its associates every day." At Continental, a landmark gesture to demonstrate leadership support was on Memorial Day, 1995, when the first Go Forward Day was held. Memorial Day is one of the airlines' busiest days. On that day, the leadership team closed the corporate office and 600 corporate workers went to the airports and did everything from serving drinks, to baggage handling, to customer interface. This gesture was so popular with employees and customers that the company still does this on several holidays.

Starting in 1997, at least twice a year in Continental's major hubs, the CEO and President hold employee meetings. These events generally attract 5,000 employees who show up to hear recaps on company accomplishments and reminders of challenges to come. The talks are followed by an hour-long question-and-answer session, the brass tacks part of the meeting. Smaller monthly meetings with employees also provide another forum for feedback. Toll-free numbers for employee suggestions and comments were installed. Since this program's inception, over 20,000 suggestions have been provided by employees.

Here are other examples of ways companies have increased leadership support and direction.

Management and the HR lead visit off-site locations to speak with employees who do not have frequent access to upper management. This is a good time for the HR team to address people's questions all at one time rather than having each person call individually or, worse,

Building Profit through Building People

remain confused about company policies and benefits. Leadership visits to remote locations not only offer direction and support, but also send a message throughout the company that everyone is valued.

The corporate CEO and presidents of SYSCO operating companies hold vision meetings twice a year with the hourly employees, administration, and operations. In this meeting, they discuss "where we are today," "where we are headed," and "where we want to be." The leaders also review STAR employer issues and try to find solutions to them. One such solution was drawing lines in parking lots to help guide drivers as they lined up their trucks to await their turns at the loading docks. This issue had become a safety hazard and a great concern to employees.

One operating company has an open-door policy for its senior management; in fact, the president keeps a bowl of chocolates by his door so that as someone stops to grab a snack, he can take the opportunity to strike up a conversation. This president also holds an operations council once every quarter during which he asks a group comprising senior vice presidents of operations, two day- and two night-warehouse staff, and two truck drivers: "What can we do to help you address barriers that prevent you from performing well?"

Another president personally calls the company's night warehouse manager twice every day, once at 10 p.m. and once at 5 a.m. He said it was worth investing his time in this critical role at a time when his company is struggling.

One of the ways in which another president fosters solidarity amongst his team is by working with the night-shift associates a couple of nights a month. This practice shows the night-shift employees that management is aware of and appreciates their hard work.

Another successful program is employee round-table meetings conducted by the CEO. Thirty employees are invited to have breakfast with the CEO and discuss issues they feel are important. The CEO speaks at the beginning of the meeting but then opens the discussion for employees' questions, ideas, comments, and so forth. Not only do these round tables increase upper management's visibility, but they also allow employees from different departments to meet and interact.

2. Strengthen Your Front-Line Supervisors

In the smoke and confusion that followed the September 11, 2001, attack on the Pentagon, dazed people looked for any way out. For many, what they heard was a booming voice calling, "Listen to me. Listen to me. Follow my voice." As reported in a number of military publications, that voice belonged to Army Lt. Col. Victor Correa, who disappeared into a wall of smoke to look for his colleagues. "Yours was the voice I heard," several people told him afterward. "All of us had different functions," Correa said, "and I knew what mine was."

What better example of the role of the front-line supervisor, who must demonstrate both competence and compassion to lead effectively? This is especially true in situations where a shortage of qualified workers has altered the face of the workplace to include inexperienced employees and some with marginal employment histories. Your front-line supervisors' understanding and acceptance of these workers is critical to their success in the workplace and, ultimately, to the company's success.

One of the most critical differentiators of SYSCO operating companies with high work-climate survey scores and low work-climate survey scores is the quality of front-line supervisors in the companies. Five of the ten most meaningful questions on the work-climate survey are directly related to front-line supervisors, and we suspect that would be true for most companies. In SYSCO's studies, the most consistent factor contributing to productivity, employee retention, good service, expense control, and safety is the effectiveness of front-line supervisors.

Frontline supervisors are crucial to developing and retaining the employees who report to them. In fact, most people do not quit a company; rather, they quit a supervisor. No matter what level they are at in the organization, if employees are not treated well by their supervisors, they end up unmotivated and uncommitted. Unfortunately, many supervisors mistakenly believe that employees are motivated only by money. That's true for some, but others are motivated by their work or by career opportunities. It is imperative that supervisors discover what motivates each worker to stay.

Operating companies have taken this principle and developed a variety of ways to implement it, described below.

They encourage frontline supervisors to rotate their own shifts so that they are available to speak with all employees.

Companies pick one day a month when the supervisor works alongside employees, perhaps riding along with a driver, working the day with a marketing associate, or stocking the warehouse.

Supervisors maintain a current job-posting location where employees can view positions in which they might be interested. Clearly communicate the qualifications needed and the person or department to contact should the associate feel qualified and interested.

Companies hold monthly meetings where supervisors are informed or updated about issues pertaining to their job. The list of topics could include ways to handle confrontation, the associate assistance program, stress management, or conflict resolution.

In addition, SYSCO has established a comprehensive plan for strengthening its frontline supervisors. Each operating company is offered tools to customize and execute the plan at its own locations on an ongoing basis. These tools are aimed at building the skills of supervisors in all aspects of management, communication, and interpersonal skills. Table 6-1 highlights the main components of the frontline supervisory development program, an ongoing 26-week program (every other week) for a full year. The table serves as a flexible model

Table 6-1. Supervisory Development Program—Rollout

Program Objective	Associated Tasks for Rollout
Identifying and Selecting Supervisors	• Identify skills needed for effective supervisors and select the top six dimensions to work on. • Design an internal recruiting strategy and post qualifications for supervisory positions in an area where all associates may view job descriptions. • Design and implement a targeted selection process.
Defining Job Descriptions for Positions Supervisors Oversee	• Supervisors and managers revise job descriptions prior to meeting. • Supervisors to complete the discussion survey. • Supervisors to meet and agree on job description.
Setting Goals and Conducting Performance Reviews	• Align activities with department and company goals. • Supervisor and manager to agree on goals. • Schedule consistent monthly goal setting and performance reviews.
Developing the Supervisor Incentive and Recognition Program	• Set incentive amounts in accordance with company focus areas. • Use incentive cost analysis to assist in identifying potential earnings. • Assist with setting the incentive/goals. • Review results weekly and pay monthly or quarterly.
Conducting Weekly One-Hour Training Sessions	• Align and schedule training topics related to priority focus areas. • Identify training facilitators by topic. • Schedule weekly one-hour training sessions.

or framework that allows the supervisors and their leaders to customize the sessions to meet the needs of the business, supervisors, and employees.

Table 6-2 provides direction for technical and operational training that can be provided to each supervisor based upon his or her experience level.

Table 6-2. Supervisory Technical/Operational Training—Rollout

Program Objective	Associated Tasks for Rollout
Understanding the Numbers	• Identify where the numbers come from. • Review last year's and current year's actual versus planned results. • Review and identify reasons for trends. • Set or review goals and how/when they will be measured.
Reviewing and Understanding the Effects and Impact	• Review the financial effects. • Identify the effects on operations and the company (other departments). • Identify the effects on the employees.
Understanding the Supervisor's Role and Responsibilities	• Identify individual activities to improve. • Identify and discuss leadership dimensions associated with activity. • Review policies and operational procedures to identify barriers. • Identify company or department initiatives to help improve.
Developing and Implementing Initiatives to Improve	• Commit to individual and group actions (written action plan). • List individual initiatives on performance review worksheet. • Identify what will be measured and when. • Review and modify initiatives timely to ensure results.

Appendix D is an outline of one lesson covered in the course on strengthening the front-line supervisor.

3. Rewards and Recognition

All employees need to know that high performance results in the kinds of rewards and recognition that they desire. The next key driver of a 5-STAR company is ensuring that the rewards and recognition system successfully identifies the best performers and provides them with both monetary and nonmonetary rewards for their exemplary performance. At SYSCO, marketing associates, district sales managers, and operating companies as a whole all strive not only to exceed the performance of their peers, but also their own personal past performances.

At Continental Airlines, effective use of rewards was a major part of the turnaround. In 1995, despite being near bankruptcy for the third time, Continental leadership gave a flat $65 reward to each employee for each month that Continental ranked in the top five of the Department of Transportation's on-time performance ratings. In the first full month of the program, the airline finished fourth, having moved up six notches from last. In the second month, Continental was in first place. That's how quickly it turned. In that first year, employees helped Continental into the top-five rankings nine times and received an extra $585 each in reward money. In 1996, Continental upped the ante: It paid employees $100 for each month that the company ranked in the top three in on-time performance, but paid nothing for fourth or fifth place.

Continental introduced similar performance incentives throughout the company. The sales force, for instance, received payments linked to gains in revenue from business travelers. Reservation agents receive bonuses based on responsibilities and the number of completed calls. As a result, the proportion of customer-reservation calls answered within 20 seconds jumped from 20% to more than 90%, the best rate in the industry. In 1996, Continental instituted a profit-sharing plan for all employees and began the attendance award program described earlier.

As SYSCO built its rewards and recognition dimension, it focused on providing ways to show its appreciation and on supporting all the other drivers of the 5-STAR model. Therefore, the company uses money, banquets, gift certificates, awards, and just about every other form of recognition possible. Whenever possible, the company tries to involve family members in the process.

For example, recognition banquets for employees and spouses (or significant others) hosted by the leadership group have proved successful in many operating companies. Such banquets also reinforce employees' sense of pride in the company. These banquets provide a forum for company leaders to recognize outstanding results and behaviors and offer an opportunity for leaders to spend informal time with their people. The reward ceremonies may be local or they may even be all-inclusive, weekend-long events. The executive team attends these functions and professional photographers take photos of employees and customers with company executives. Awards have ranged from plaques, to Swiss watches, to diamond rings for truly stellar associates.

One of the most popular events is the "Haul of Champions" National Truck Roadeo, an event designed to reward top warehouse and distribution employees and to demonstrate top management's support and appreciation of delivery and warehouse staff. The "roadeo" is a truck driving and warehousing competition that culminates a year-long program to recognize those with outstanding performance. Each operating company holds a local competition, and the top competitors are selected for the national competition. The national roadeo consists of an all-expense-paid weekend for associates and their spouses. There is a barbecue during which the winners of the previous year triumphantly enter riding Brahma bulls and longhorn steers. The night ends with one of country music's best performers. The following day is the competition among the "Best of the Best."

Many of the operating companies have dramatically improved employee satisfaction and financial performance by paying for performance that directly affects business results. In some cases, for example, employees are paid for the accomplishment of results rather than just the time spent the job. This activity-based compensation program is discussed in detail in Chapter 8.

4. Inclusion for Engagement and Diversity

When employees sense that the company trusts them enough to share information about its performance, they become engaged. This sharing equips employees with the knowledge they need about what needs to be improved if the company is to succeed and empowers them to be involved in decision-making. Inclusion of employees also demonstrates that *all* associates are equally part of the company, regardless of their race, color, religion, or any other characteristic that has the potential to divide people.

Carl Frost, the renowned consultant, often opens his presentations by asking the assembled group, "What day is it?" The point of the question is that if one does not know what day it is—whether it's the 15th of January in frigid Ithaca, New York, or August 15th in steamy Houston, Texas—then one does not know how to prepare for the environment. Wearing a full parka in Houston during August will result in the same level of discomfort as wearing shorts and a tank top in Ithaca in January. Continually sharing information with employees helps them understand "what day it is" in the company's competitive environment.

In 1995, at Continental one of the early on landmark gestures convinced employees that everyone was in the turnaround effort together. The HR lead and a group of executives and employees hauled a cart full of 800-page "corporate policy and procedure" books out to the parking lot and ceremonially torched them in front of a large employee audience. This symbolic gesture signaled a new attitude about engagement. Then, a taskforce of employees and executives streamlined the 800-page book to an 80-page, user friendly document that was mailed to all employees.

Another key to engagement at Continental was communication. In fact, improved communication was one of the key points of the Go Forward plan. Every single work day, employees can peruse a one-page company newsletter for updates on the previous day's performance, for news on company's activities, and for information on how the stock performed. The newsletter is burst-faxed to 350 locations and e-mailed to 2,000 locations from Tokyo to Düsseldorf, Madrid and Montreal, and everywhere in between. The newsletter is also read on voice mail for people to dial in and listen.

In 1996, to ignite more interest in the company's monthly newsletter, *Continental Times*, the company revamped it *USA Today*-style and then added the *Continental Quarterly* to profile the softer side of employee workforce issues. These changes worked to help communicate the change in the culture of the company and show that people are having fun in the workplace.

The communication framework that was instrumental in Continental's turnaround in the late 1990's still exists today (see Table 6-3).

Involving and engaging associates while leveraging diversity has been accomplished in SYSCO operating companies in a variety of ways.

Companies keep associates informed as to how well the company is doing, where it is headed, what the company's goals are, and how the company will get there. Some operating companies hold town hall meetings fortnightly, at which they share information and highlight the statistics on the diversity of their workplace.

Companies maintain a bulletin board where corporate newsletters, press releases, birthday announcements, and anniversaries can be posted so that associates are kept in the loop.

Many companies set up a suggestion box to elicit and reward ideas that may lead to increases in productivity, improved safety, and so forth.

A stunning example of leveraging diversity occurred in an operating company whose management recognized that the Latino population in its market had grown significantly over the previous five years. The leadership hired a bilingual HR manager and bilingual front-line supervisors to better attract and retain their workforce. The results were phenomenal, especially in night-shift warehouse operations, with retention improving from 10% to 65% in six months.

Table 6-3. Communication Framework Used in the 1990s, Continental

Tool	Frequency	Description
		Ongoing Communications
Daily News	Daily	Newsletter to all employees (hard copy and E-mail)
Voice mail update from chief executive	Weekly	CEO records a new message each Friday
Continental Times	Monthly	4-page newsletter (*USA Today*-style)
Continental Quarterly	Quarterly	50-page journal (more comprehensive articles than in *Continental Times*)
Videocassettes	At least 3 times a year	Stories of the state of the business and plans for the future
		Special Communications
Employee meetings	3 times a year	Meetings with employees at all 8 locations
Q & A's	2 times a year	Follow-up reports in response to employees' questions; questions are invited from all employees in writing or to a toll-free telephone number in the corporate communications department; answers are from CEO, COO, or VP-HR
Division roundtables	1-2 times a year	Skip-level meetings for each division
Communication surveys	Annually	Employees' ratings of their directors' and vice presidents' communications during past year; used in computing each manager's bonus
Payroll stuffers	As needed	Pay-related announcements, for example on profit sharing
Open-house meetings	Monthly	Open forum discussions with employees from all locations of the company; led by CEO, COO, and VP-HR

Building Profit through Building People

5. Address Your Employees' Quality of Life

Employees want a nice, comfortable work environment. They also want to have a job that does not unnecessarily interfere with their families or other leisure pursuits. Addressing employees' quality of life helps to improve and maintain an organization's ability to attract, motivate, and retain the most talented people in the industry. Creating a work environment where employees feel comfortable and want to come to work each day often requires attending to local organizational conditions, rather than rolling out a corporate one-size-fits-all policy.

SYSCO encourages its operating companies to think innovatively about ways to encourage a positive quality of life. Some examples follow.

Companies implement a casual dress day, especially during the warmer months, and especially in warm locations.

Leaders develop an associate referral program where referrals that lead to permanent hires are rewarded monetarily.

Employees are allowed to combine sick and vacation days into all-purpose leave, so workers can take the time off for whatever personal reasons they choose. Associates often have family events (for example, parent-teacher meetings, and children's school events) or other responsibilities that can only be addressed during normal work hours. Rather than encouraging people to lie in order to use sick leave, this policy lets them fulfill their obligations openly and honestly.

Overview

Implementing the 5-STAR model takes effort, persistence, and creativity. Some of the efforts may engage all parts of the company in similar ways, whereas others emerge from within a local business unit or a work-unit, based on the needs and desires of employees. The balance and blend between corporate programs and the innovative programs developed and managed at the business-unit level is what has enabled SYSCO companies to build loyalty to the larger corporation while eliciting strong affiliation with the local workplace. In Chapter 9, we will explore how these local innovations can be shared across companies to allow all operating units to learn from the others.

RECAP

1. Five basic steps go into building a STAR management model:
   - Strategic planning
   - Goal setting
   - Assessing the current state
   - Interpreting and prioritizing
   - Implementing programs for improvement
2. The dimensions of a 5-STAR company are divided into four basic performance areas:
   - Financial
   - Customer
   - Operational
   - Human Capital

CHAPTER 7

Testing the 5-STAR Model

In Chapter 6, we discussed associate satisfaction as a key factor behind a company's continuing success. We described the processes used to set goals, assess the current state, interpret and prioritize, create infrastructure, and monitor progress with regard to becoming a 5-STAR employer. Much of this effort focused on the work-climate survey emphasizing how to use climate-survey results to improve the workplace. Although we implicitly recognized the assumption that improving climate leads to improved business results, that assumption was neither described nor proven.

In this chapter we will show how to gather, analyze, and act on data to test the accuracy of the theory implicit in the balanced scorecard— that there is a connection between improved climate and improved business results. To do so, we will more explicitly describe how we believe that being a 5-STAR company results in better business results and then show how we have looked at SYSCO's internal data to test this assumption.

Testing the Model's Theories

Of course, many companies conduct annual climate surveys. But the often-neglected key to good management is to link those climate survey results directly to employee retention, operating performance, customer satisfaction, and profitability. Additionally, a company must continue to analyze which practices result in the desired behaviors and satisfaction levels of associates.

Returning to the balanced scorecard, Figure 6-1 on page 74, note a few of the major drivers. There are a number of monthly performance indicators that SYSCO tracks across the operating companies. All of these indicators are listed on the scorecard, and how these measures relate to one another probably describes how the company succeeds.

Having a theory of how a firm succeeds, however, does not mean that the theory is accurate. This is why it is necessary to put a premium on analyzing internal data to determine if assumptions about how the business succeeds are actually correct.

Within the human capital domain, we presuppose that satisfied employees are far less likely to leave, thereby contributing to high rates of retention. We also suggest that when employees are satisfied, it is likely that they engage in and are more productive in their jobs, are more likely to go beyond their specified roles to help others, and are less likely to engage in counterproductive behaviors such as theft or vandalism. We assume that satisfied employees serve customers better, and that when all of this happens, organizations will have lower expenses and higher profits.

If these assumptions and beliefs are correct, we would expect to find empirical relationships among the measures collected. SYSCO has collected three years' worth of information on thousands of employees in hundreds of jobs across many of its operating companies. Below we look at these data to test our theories about the importance of climate as an integral piece of company success. Let's take a look at the careful process and the data used to test the hypotheses about the importance of work climate and employee satisfaction.

Data Collection and the Analytical Process

SYSCO's climate-survey process consists of surveying each company every 18 months. (See Appendix C for the 2004 work-climate survey.) In keeping with the commitment to its companies' entrepreneurial spirit, operating companies are allowed to choose from two different survey times each year. The survey research center at Cornell University analyzes all the data, but the process is still time consuming; companies must take at least 20% of their associates off the job to complete the 30-minute survey. Because some companies are busiest in the fall and others are busiest in the spring, each operating company could decide when it wanted to participate. The surveys started with just a few companies, where management voluntarily decided to participate and was willing to pay for the survey. Over time, the process has become integral to the management of the business, and beginning in 2003 all of the operating companies began to participate.

SYSCO also conducts different types of customer satisfaction surveys each year. (See Appendix A.) For these surveys, staff at Cornell's survey research center print the surveys, mail them to top customers, and enter and analyze all the data. Because management expends no time or effort in this survey process, all operating companies participate at the same time.

In addition, starting in 1998 SYSCO began tracking and recording internal company metrics (quality, productivity, shrinkage, operating expenses, pretax profit, and so forth) for every one of the operating companies.

One important factor for conducting a data-analysis is making sure that the data are matched appropriately. For instance, because the customer satisfaction survey is conducted in between the two alternative seasons for gathering the employee climate-survey data, it is important to ensure that only *previous* climate data are related to customer satisfaction. To rush the analyses, some business leaders are prone to relating a climate measure in the fall to the current retention data. However, because the current retention data report *past retention,* tying those figures to current climate is illogical; those who were dissatisfied would have departed, so they would not be able to participate in the climate survey. For instance, the attitudes of people who left between January and June cannot possibly be related to a survey conducted in June. Consequently, it is crucial to take great care to present conservative analyses, always tying climate measures to *later* measures of retention, customer satisfaction, and so forth.

The Results

Let's return to the value-profit chain we discussed in Chapter 2. Remember that the model proposed that employee satisfaction drives both customer satisfaction and operational excellence, and that these relate to profitability (where, obviously, profitability is a function of revenues minus costs). This generic model underlies the 5-STAR mode and guides some of the thinking in how to assess its validity.

Table 7-1 highlights some of the results of SYSCO's analysis by correlating elements of the value-profit chain with solid business results. Across the board, you can see significant differences in performance between companies that scored in the top 25% in terms of work climate scores compared with companies that scored in the bottom 25%. The top 25% operating companies shared a number of common best practices and areas of high performance, as described in the following sections.

Table 7-1. Value-Profit Chain Correlations, SYSCO*

	Work Climate Score Avg.+	Customer Satisfaction Score Avg.+	Marketing Associate Retention %	Driver Retention %	Worker's Compensation, % of Sales
Top 25%	4.00	4.03	85.8%	88.7%	0.07%
Bottom 25%	3.58	4.02	72.7%	78.7%	0.20%
Variance (Points)	0.42	0.01	13.1%	10.0%	0.13%

*Numbers and percentages are representative, not actual. Comparisons and trends are accurate.
+Out of a possible 5.00

Climate and Human Capital

First, in a customer service business long-term personal relationships between the sales representative and the customer distinguish excellent from mediocre companies. For this reason, SYSCO places tremendous emphasis on its ability to retain marketing associates. Drivers (who have direct contact with the customers) and warehouse personnel (who prepare the deliveries) are also critical to keeping customers satisfied because they are the ones who truly know how to serve customers. When those individuals know what customers want and expect, the result is satisfied customers and a competitive edge.

If the 5-STAR model is valid, we would expect that satisfied employees would be more likely to stay than would less satisfied employees. As we look across our companies, we find that exact result. As you can see in Table 7-2, companies with satisfied warehouse staff, drivers, and marketing associates do exhibit higher retention rates among each of those jobs than companies with less satisfied employees.

Climate and Operations

That climate relates to retention is great, but as we all know, it is irrelevant if that retention does not have an impact on important opera-

Table 7-2. Employee Retention Increases with Higher Climate Survey Scores, SYSCO*

	Top 25% Fiscal Year '04 Climate Score	Lowest 25% Fiscal Year '04 Climate Score	Percentage Point Difference
Marketing Associates	91%	82%	9
Delivery Staff	87%	78%	9
Night Warehouse Workers	72%	34%	38

*Numbers and percentages are representative, not actual. Comparisons and trends are accurate.

tions measures. When employees are satisfied with and committed to their companies, they strive to see their company succeed. On a positive note, this means that they will efficiently and effectively perform their jobs, resulting in high productivity and quality. These employees also are less likely to engage in counterproductive activities such as theft or sabotage.

SYSCO was able to relate climate scores to the measures of labor productivity, quality (pieces per error), and theft or sabotage. Labor productivity is measured by the number of hours worked per case of goods delivered. (Thus a low number means the company is not very productive as it takes a lot of hours for each case.) Quality is assessed by examining the number of pieces that are shipped relative to each error. (Thus a high ratio means a company performs well.) Shrinkage—assessed as the number of cases lost, spoiled, or damaged relative to the total number of cases—measures the care with which associates handle inventory. These measures all related to climate: Companies that have high levels of employee satisfaction are the ones that also tend to exhibit the highest levels of performance on these operational measures.

Climate and Customers

That satisfied associates deliver the best customer service seems obvious. Sears' experience with its service-profit chain and several academ-

Building Profit through Building People

ic studies have supported this basic relationship (Rafaeli, 1989; Rogg, Schmidt, Shull, & Schmitt, 2001; Schlesinger & Zornitsky, 1991; Schmit & Allscheid, 1995; Schneider & Bowen, 1985; Schneider, White, & Paul, 1998). However, simply believing in one's heart that the 5-STAR model is true is not enough in the business world. As can be seen in Figure 7-1, companies with the highest levels of employee satisfaction also tend to be the companies with the highest levels of customer satisfaction.

Climate and Financial Performance

Thus far the discussion has highlighted how employee satisfaction drives retention, operational performance, and customer satisfaction. However, while not unimportant to shareholders, certainly financial performance serves as the most important criteria they look at. Consequently, the 5-STAR model's effectiveness can best be assessed by examining the relationship between employee satisfaction and financial performance.

At SYSCO, companies with the highest levels of employee satisfaction are those that also display the highest levels of performance in terms of both controlling costs (operating expenses) and profitability (net operating profit). So when satisfied employees stay with the organization and provide great customer service, increased profitability almost inevitably results. Satisfied employees work harder and smarter to deliver efficient and effective service to customers. These employees keep operational costs down while maximizing sales from customers.

Overview

The previous chapters have detailed how the 5-STAR management model was developed and implemented. The 5-STAR model, however, is essentially a theory of the business, and any theory must be tested for its usefulness. The next generation of human resources requires taking an analytical approach and being willing to be held accountable for business results.

If you really want to build your company into a 5-STAR one, you need to collect the data that prove that your model works and to demonstrate accountability. This does not mean that the results will always come out exactly as you expect. In fact, sometimes the climate scores may not correlate significantly with the customer satisfaction ratings.

Whether the data correlate significantly or not, the important point is that without data, it is impossible to know if what you are doing is right, and if it is not, how to improve. That road leads to failure for organizations and for our HR professionals as leaders.

RECAP:

1. Many companies have done climate surveys for decades.
2. What is critical to the ability to leverage performance is ensuring that the survey results are linked in a meaningful way to the critical success factors of the business.
3. Data do show that satisfied employees:
   - Stay longer.
   - Are more productive and do higher quality work.
   - Better satisfy customers.
   - Increase profit by keeping costs down and maximizing revenue.

CHAPTER 8

Embedding the 5-STAR Model

In previous chapters, we discussed how to develop a 5-STAR model that provides an understanding of how the business works, how to build the programs and process to execute the model, and how to measure the key indicators to test the validity of the model. In this chapter, we will explore how to begin embedding the model in your organization, using SYSCO's experience as a case study.

While this case study is a useful guide, it is crucial to ground the process of embedding the model in your own company's structure and culture. Some organizations are highly structured and centralized, with processes and practices that are uniform throughout. Others are loose confederations of entities. Companies' cultures vary widely, from creative to all-business, from risk-averse to daredevil, and everything in between.

There is, however, *one* challenge shared by every company, regardless of structure and culture: getting managers to actually buy in to new programs. Often managers resist acting on concepts such as value-profit chains (VPCs) or the 5-STAR model. While the ideas sound great in theory, the managers simply are not convinced that such approaches actually have an effect on the bottom line. In most organizations, the corporate office can declare by fiat that managers must implement the concepts and hold them accountable for their actions. Consequently, the business can execute the model through incentives and coercion, with only the hope that at some point managers will individually and personally adopt the basic concepts as their own. Sadly enough, this approach often results in resistance and failure for a model or practice that could have succeeded and benefited the business. Given this universal challenge, SYSCO's experience of embedding the model within a decentralized, entrepreneurial environment may be especially applicable.

How to Embed the Model

SYSCO used a market-based approach to embedding the model. Under this approach, each business unit only used the corporate resources it was willing to actually pay for, thereby encouraging corporate staff to act entrepreneurially in developing programs. Using this market-based framework required corporate staff to adhere to four basic principles:

1. *Allow for free choice.* Provide the services the operating companies— the internal customers—want rather than force them to accept what you think they need.
2. *Data sells.* Focus on collecting the data that will help the internal customers succeed in their businesses.
3. *Learn from winners.* Identify the units that are most successful and study them to discover what drives their success.
4. *Demonstrate impact.* Collect the data that show the bottom-line impact of the programs.

Here is how these principles served as a foundation for embedding the 5-STAR model.

Building Profit through Building People

Freedom of Choice Builds Ownership

SYSCO has a decentralized structure and entrepreneurial culture. The organization's operating principle of earned autonomy provides both a sense of ownership for business leaders and an opportunity for each unit to innovate with few corporate mandates. However, getting the operating companies to adopt the 5-STAR model in this environment presented a whole host of challenges. The earned autonomy philosophy prevented the corporate office from mandating almost anything, particularly anything as individual as how to manage people. The decentralized decision-making structure required a different approach: persuasion as opposed to coercion. The model could not be mandated, and business leaders could never be coerced into adopting it.

This entrepreneurial spirit was one reason that testing the 5-STAR model was so important. The burden fell on the corporate staff to provide indisputable data that the model would help leaders improve their business results.

Interestingly, this approach actually facilitated the success of the model. When the business leaders voluntarily adopted a model or practice (as opposed to having it forced on them), they had a vested interest in seeing it succeed. The freedom to choose eliminated the option of blaming failure on someone else: "I knew it would never work. But you know how corporate gets these stupid ideas in their heads." So, while the approach entailed greater up-front costs in terms of data gathering, communications, and so forth, it also increased the likelihood of successful implementation.

Theory Builds Belief, but Data Drive Action

The VPC model provides an intuitively appealing framework for understanding the importance of employee loyalty to business success. Although theory is great for getting intellectual acceptance, it does not always "sell" in terms of driving real behavioral change. Eliciting different behaviors (meaning resource allocation, communications, investment of time, etc.) requires convincing data that the behavioral change will have a significant payoff.

Chapter 7 presented the bulk of the information SYSCO gathered over a three-year period that provided analytical and empirical data demonstrating the value of the model. The next task was to get this information into the hands and heads of those who needed it. This was done in a multistep process.

First, as the work-climate data flowed in, they were quickly tied to operational performance measures. Time was of the essence, as one could always argue that results from one or two years ago might not be relevant to today's challenges. Second, as the empirical support became available, the road shows began. The corporate HR staff tried to get onto the agendas of each region's quarterly planning meeting, which brought together all of the business unit leaders within a region. These meetings provided opportunities for business leaders to see the relationships between the climate scores and the operational performance measures upon which their companies were being evaluated. By first learning about the model at the regional meetings, as opposed to the national one, leaders were exposed to the data in a more personal setting. In addition, this smaller setting enabled much more experience-sharing, as leaders who had implemented the model could provide testimonials to its success in their businesses. Finally, and to some extent, most importantly, such a setting lent much less of a corporately mandated aura to the ideas. It made leaders feel as if they had a choice in the matter, and they felt greater ownership of the process.

This process effectively built a desire among a number of the leaders to implement the 5-STAR model. Certainly a number of skeptical leaders saw this model (and still do) as another fad that would simply blow over in time. However, a core of early adopters was able to gain traction in building their organizations and achieving improved business results, although doing so required some preliminary tools.

Learn from the Winners

Having built the compelling desire among many of the leaders by demonstrating the business case for implementing the 5-STAR model, the next challenge was to provide tools and techniques to help them do so successfully. Given the relatively small corporate HR staff, this quickly became significant. If leaders did not have the tools and techniques readily available, the initiative would soon fail due to lack of follow-through. Therefore, priority was placed on developing a satisfactory, albeit suboptimal, set of tools and suggestions that leaders could use as guides for implementing the model.

Based on results of the work-climate surveys, the corporate staff quickly separated the highest 5-STAR companies (the top 25%) from the lowest performing companies (the bottom 25%) and tried to identify some of the practices that distinguished them from one another. This process entailed understanding the drivers of low scores, so the first step was to identify the particular survey items that best differentiated the top and bottom companies. This led to picking out what became known as the 14 most "impactful" items, as shown in Table 8-1.

The second task was to determine some of the specific leadership and management practices that distinguished the top from the bottom companies. This process required additional data gathering, including a number of interviews with the HR and operations leaders of these businesses. A number of practices were identified, and then the 5-STAR team sat down and tried to make the conceptual links between the practices and the dimensions. Note that this was not empirically based: The team did not know for a fact that a particular practice tied directly to a particular dimension. Rather, what was known was that the practices tended to be associated with the high-performance com-

Table 8-1. The Work-Climate Survey's 14 Most "Impactful" Items, SYSCO

5-STAR Dimension	Work Climate Survey Item
Leadership Support	A1: I know what is expected of me at work.
	A6: I know the business goals of the company.
	A9: Upper management (e.g., president, executive vice president) spends time talking with employees about our business direction.
Front-Line Supervisor	B1: My supervisor treats me with dignity and respect.
	B6: My supervisor and I review my top goals and discuss how they contribute to the company's success.
	B8: I have received constructive feedback on my performance within the last six months.
	B12: My supervisor removes obstacles so I can do my job better.
Quality of Life	C1: I trust what the company tells me.
	C4: Different departments of our company work together to get the job done.
Rewards	E2: My pay is the same or better than other companies in our market.
	E4: Doing my job well leads to monetary rewards.
	E7: Decisions made about promotions or job changes within this organization are fair.
Engagement/ Diversity	F1: I am willing to work harder to help this company succeed.
	F2: I am proud to work for SYSCO.

panies and, conceptually, it appeared that the particular practice would most likely have an impact on a particular climate dimension.

The initial goal was to provide at least three suggestions for how businesses could improve their climate scores on each of the five dimensions. Table 8-2 provides an example of the kinds of best-practice ideas provided to leaders about how they could improve their climate scores. This kind of a quick-hit tool enabled business leaders to make some high-impact changes in their organizations and to do so quickly.

Table 8-2. 5-STAR Dimensions—Best Practices, SYSCO

Leadership Support	Coaching and Maximizing Performance	State of the Company Address	Monthly Senior Management Meetings
Front-Line Supervisor	Strengthen Front-Line Supervisor Program	Monthly Supervisory Meetings	e-learning "Super" in Front-Line Supervisor
Quality of Life	Clean Warehouse and Trucks	Open-Door Policy	Family Gatherings
Rewards	Execute Activity-Based Compensation	Competitive Pay to Market	Career Opportunities
Engagement/Diversity	Comprehensive Orientation Process	Targeted Selection	Leadership Roundtable Meetings with Associates

Over time, the tools became more sophisticated as more information was gathered and leaders of the businesses felt empowered to innovate in how they built their 5-STAR companies. Having built the quick-hit tools, the next phase was to develop an even deeper analysis of what constitutes a 5-STAR company and provide more detailed and valuable guidance to business leaders regarding how they could create such a business.

This goal led to the development of a how-to guide for leaders wishing to move their organizations forward within the 5-STAR framework. It provided a step-by-step process for them to follow and offered some specific suggestions about how to improve their climate scores on each of the dimensions.

Remember, every climate dimension is made up of multiple items, some of which have been identified among the most "impactful." Experience and data have confirmed the kinds of leadership practices that can drive improved dimension scores, and conceptually, one can trace each practice to the items to which it would most directly tie.

Consequently, the guidebook provides this information in an easy-to-use and easy-to-apply format. Appendix E identifies and describes some of the practices and programs—5-STAR actions—that are included in the Guidebook and are likely to achieve high impact on each of the 5-STAR dimensions.

Demonstrate Impact

So far we have focused on the first-generation data, that is, the data that related climate scores to important internal performance metrics and served to garner buy-in from business leaders for the basic model. However, once the business leaders bought into the model, the second-generation data came into play. These data focused on demonstrating the impact of the tools that were offered in the guidebook.

Demonstrating impact is important for a number of reasons. First, the early generation of tools was based on conjecture and extrapolation. Although they made intuitive sense and in some cases were backed up by anecdotal data, good data helped to identify which tools really had impact. This information prevented the organizations from investing in areas that would not pay off. Second, the data increased the credibility of those seeking to implement the 5-STAR model. If business leaders had bought into the model but could not find a way to improve their own unit's performance, then both the model and those who developed it became useless in the leaders' minds.

ABC—An Example of Impact

In the next chapter we will provide a description of how SYSCO used the basic 5-STAR approach coupled with a shared best practice portal to increase safety performance and generate considerable cost savings to the corporation. However, here we describe how the model worked with regard to improving both the business climate and retention among delivery drivers.

Delivery drivers serve as almost secondary ambassadors to the customer. At one level, drivers' friendly interactions with customers help to cement the impression that the company is a supplier that customers enjoy doing business with. But in the restaurant business, having a friendly driver means nothing if the order is wrong or does not arrive on time. The customers need to know that they will get what they want, when they want it, in order to maintain an effective inventory. In large part, making sure that the restaurants always have enough to serve, never too much to go to waste, is the responsibility of the delivery drivers.

In examining the winners and losers in terms of both climate and performance, an interesting trend emerged. A number of the winners had adopted an activity-based compensation (ABC) program for the drivers. Under a traditional hourly compensation program, the only way drivers could make more money is to work overtime, and the best way to work overtime is to waste time. Wasting time by taking long breaks and so forth not only results in less productivity (because the company pays more money for the same amount of work), but also results in orders arriving late to customers—a double whammy. Under an ABC system, the company augments the basic pay rate with incentives for drivers who complete more deliveries, make fewer mistakes, and maintain good safety records.

In studying the winners, it soon became apparent that the companies that had adopted ABC systems had higher quality-of-life scores among their drivers than the others did. The ABC system quickly became a tool that was made available to all the other companies. Every company that implemented ABC had significantly higher satisfaction among drivers in the first year. In addition, the retention rate rose 8%, delivery expenses dropped, and customer satisfaction levels improved. As the ABC system has been adopted by more and more companies, similar positive outcomes resulted each time, and these outcomes are experienced by both union and non-union companies.

In essence, this experience undeniably demonstrated the value of an innovative management practice throughout the whole VPC. The ABC practice drove higher employee satisfaction, which resulted in decreased costs and increased customer satisfaction, both of which translated into a profitable business.

Overview

Using a market-based framework for internal operations can increase both the efficiency and effectiveness of programs and their implementation. By allowing leaders freedom to choose whether to adopt the 5-STAR model, using data to elicit action, providing tools to help them implement the model, and demonstrating how the tools improve performance, SYSCO has persuaded its companies to almost universally embed the 5-STAR approach more rapidly than would ever have happened via corporate mandate.

RECAP

1. Allowing business leaders the freedom to choose whether to adopt a 5-STAR model encourages success where it is adopted, and success provides incentive for non-adopters to voluntarily adopt it later.
2. Providing good data encourages adopters not only to believe the model, but also to act on it.
3. The model and data provide the end goal, but you have to provide tools that can move the organization toward that goal.
4. Don't stop with the tools; gather more data to determine the effectiveness of the tools.

CHAPTER 9

Building Dynamic 5-STAR Capability

The last few chapters provided a detailed description of the process used to develop, execute, test, and embed a 5-STAR model. However, as the competitive environment exhibits constant and sometimes rapid change, companies must create the capability for a dynamic 5-STAR model. In this chapter, we discuss how to select metrics to measure success and how to develop an information infrastructure—a best business practices (BBP) Web portal—that facilitates sharing knowledge regarding innovative practices for building successful organizations.

Best Practices ... but for How Long?

Current thinking in the field of people-management often focuses on a set of practices that, if implemented, would purportedly drive higher performance. Authors such as Pfeffer (1998) argue that practices such as selective staffing, training, job security, information sharing, and so forth comprise such "best practices" that should be universally implemented in organizations. Two problems exist with such prescriptions: a lack of specificity and the risk of stagnation.

We do not disagree that at a general level there are some principles that can and should be implemented by organizations seeking
competitive advantage through their people. Because employees
need to be skilled, selective staffing and training programs can provide benefits to the organization. Because employees must be motivated to do their work right, pay for performance can be beneficial.
And because employees need to do the right things, information
sharing and participation can result in significant returns for an
organization.

Nevertheless, such general guidance is of little use when your organization seeks to actually develop and implement a specific practice that
would significantly improve performance. For example, selection tests
at hiring can be great, but if they measure the wrong characteristics
they could hurt the organization. Training programs can develop the
wrong skills or be conducted with little positive impact. Pay-for-
performance systems can result in dysfunctional outcomes. And
encouraging participation by an unskilled or dissatisfied workforce
could hinder, rather than facilitate, performance. Consequently, any
effective strategy for managing people must present practices that have
been proven successful and have been articulated at a level of specificity such that users know exactly what to do.

In addition, while the principles may endure over time, the efficacy of specific practices seldom does. The influence of innovative practices often exhibits a short half-life as the excitement and newness
wear off. When customers, competitors, and markets change, even the
most enduring, high-impact practices and systems can end up providing no, or even negative, value. A few years ago a senior line executive
at a *Fortune* 100 company described the alignment of the management practices at the company as "extremely well aligned with each
other....The problem is that they are all aligned around a strategy that
no longer exists" (Wright, McMahan, Snell, & Gerhart, 1997). You
need to stop doing the practices that are not working before you can

implement newer, better practices. Stated another way: If the horse is dead, don't get on it!

Consequently, among the challenges inherent in building an enduring 5-STAR company is that of creating an infrastructure that provides specific information to those who need it when they need it, that encourages participants to innovate and create new ways of implementing the model, and that enables sharing that information as quickly as possible.

SYSCO's response to these challenges was to build a best business practices (BBP) intranet Web portal. In the next section, we examine how this infrastructure was designed to keep information on productive management practices up to date and to enable managers to access knowledge about practices that could improve their companies' performances.

Defining a Valid Set of Metrics

The first step toward creating an information infrastructure is to define the metrics that would drive the definitions of success.

What do we mean by a "valid" set of metrics? Every measure has some level of inaccuracy. Industrial psychologists refer to the ideas of "contamination" and "deficiency" to describe the inaccuracy of an individual measure. Contamination means that a measure might be affected by factors outside the company's control. For instance, measuring revenue or revenue growth seems to be an obviously valid measure. However, different geographic locations have different socioeconomic conditions, and often there is variation in how these conditions change. Comparing the revenues or revenue growth of a company in an economically depressed region with a company in an economically vibrant region is unfair because those companies' revenues are impacted by a contaminating factor—the local economy.

Deficiency in a measure means that the measure misses some important aspect of performance. For instance, net profitability, although definitely important, might be deficient in that the profit could be achieved in the short term by reducing investments or cutting costs that directly relate to satisfying customers. So, simply to track profitability misses important aspects of an organization's overall long-term performance.

In light of these challenges, SYSCO sought to develop an integrated set of metrics that, on the whole, represented all the important areas of business-unit performance. Building on the thinking of the balanced scorecard (Kaplan & Norton, 1996), management selected four areas—customer, financial, operational, and human capital—that would guide the company's specific metrics. Six key measures within each of the four areas were identified to track and publish on a monthly basis. Although 24 measures may seem excessive, this number was necessary in order to provide a valid set of metrics to guide decisions. While any one measure might have been deficient, the *whole set* was not deficient. And the set comprised measures over which business leaders exerted considerable control. (That is, they were not contaminated.) These measures are listed in Figure 6-1.

Using the Metrics to Focus Attention

At a general level, the purpose of a metrics model is to focus decision makers' attention on key measures of performance. More specifically, at SYSCO, however, after considerable examination of the variations in performance across the businesses on each of the metrics, the decision was made to set the general objective of continuous improvement, with a measurable goal of reducing the gaps between the lowest and highest performing companies. Helping companies reach this goal entailed three basic ideas:

Building Profit through Building People

1. Provide a broad overview of past performance as well as potentially predictive results in the four major components of the business.
2. Provide a benchmark of performance and target gap-reduction in macro (four general areas) and micro (specific performance metrics) measures.
3. Link best practices and best-practice companies in the high-performance areas so that management in other companies could learn from and use them as a basis for performance improvement.

Building User-Friendly Communication of Best Practices

With a metrics model in place and a goal for the model accepted, the next step is to enable and encourage communications. Like many other concepts in the value-profit chain, implementing and sharing best business practices is not as simple as it sounds. It is all too easy to construct a sophisticated, complex system of sharing and see it collapse under its own weight. And there are many obstacles to why best-practice concepts that work for one company or department do *not* work for another. It is important to success to provide a high-quality tool or service that adds value for your internal corporate customers.

To institutionalize the importance of knowing and applying management practices for every associate at every operating company, SYSCO elicited the support of senior-management leadership for creating an information infrastructure to ensure success and establish a best-business-practices champion at each company location. With the proper support in place, a user-friendly communication technology then was developed to enable employees at all levels to use and leverage the tool, which was also linked to various reward programs.

SYSCO's communication approach was to build a best business practices (BBP) intranet Web portal that would provide the platform for organizational improvement. Creating this Web architecture entailed creating the basic framework for managers to both share information on their organization's successful practices and to learn from other organizations' contributions.

When business units perform in the top quartile of the company in an organizational area, they are encouraged to share on the BBP portal the practices that they believe drove their performance. They are guided through a process in which they describe:

- The quantitative or qualitative improvement realized from the practice: "We reduced accidents by 20% within two months."
- Three contributing factors that facilitated the implementation and effectiveness of the practice: "We already had a high level of trust with workers, so they embraced the change."
- The details of the practice: "We developed a formal feedback mechanism whereby the frequency of safe and unsafe behaviors is posted each week."
- The potential stumbling blocks: "Although employees supported it, we faced difficulty in getting supervisors to buy in."
- Information regarding whom to contact for detailed information about the practice and for answers to any further questions.

Using the BBP Web Portal: A Safety Example

"Power users" of the BBP Web portal can use an advanced search feature to drill down to the information they seek quickly. Figure 9-1 shows such a search page.

But there are many ways to get information from the portal, which has four levels. To illustrate in detail how it works, what follows is an example of how you, as safety manager at a company, might use the BBP Web site to find ways to increase safety at your location.

Figure 9-1. BBP Portal Power Search, SYSCO

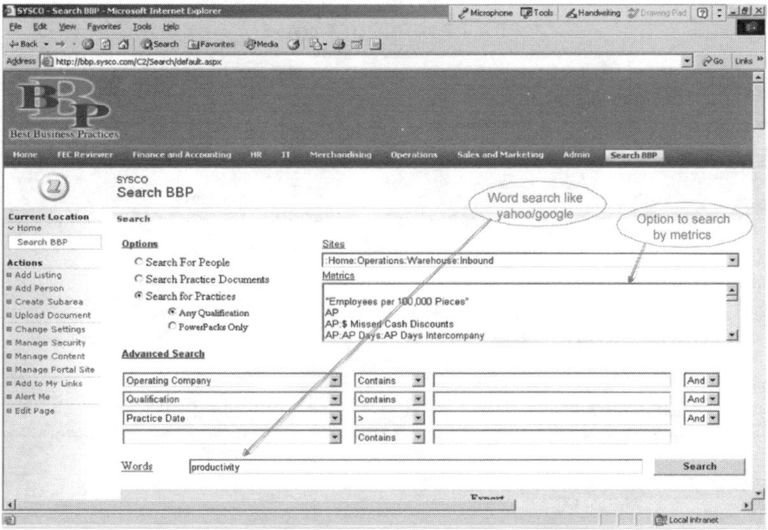

Choose an Organizational Area

As previously discussed, four organizational areas—financial, customer, human capital, and operational—are the overall guiding framework. So, the vice president of marketing at any business might first connect to the customer area of the BBP Web portal, whereas the vice president of finance might first connect to the financial area. Since your goal—improving safety—clearly relates to the human capital area, you would first click on the human capital icon, as shown in Figure 9-2.

This selection goes to the first level of metrics. The metrics for the organizational area represent a weighted composite of the five metrics that compose that area. Figure 9-3 illustrates how these composite scores are presented with both normative data (top quartile, median, bottom quartile) and individual company scores and ranks.

Figure 9-2. BBP Portal Organizational Areas, SYSCO

BEST PRACTICE DATABASE

CORE BUSINESS PRACTICES	KEY METRICS REPORT
FINANCIAL	JOIN A COMMUNITY OF PRACTICE
CUSTOMER	CENTRAL TRAINING SCHEDULE
HUMAN CAPITAL	SEARCH
OPERATIONAL	

Select Key Metrics

Within the human capital area, the second level provides the five performance metrics associated with that area. Historical data up to the present month are available across the corporation on each of the metrics. The level of worker's compensation claims is one clear metric of safety. So, clicking on the worker's compensation button (Figure 9-4), you would be presented with your unit's monthly performance on this metric compared to all the other units over the past two years. This makes it possible for you to identify just how far your unit's performance deviates from peers' performance.

Choose Key Drivers

Assuming the performance gap is quite large, the next step is to connect to the key drivers of performance. Therefore, the portal provides

Building Profit through Building People

Figure 9-3. BBP Portal Key Metrics All Areas, SYSCO

▨ = 25th quartile

▨ = 75th quartile

	CUSTOMER		HUMAN CAPITAL		FINANCIAL		OPERATIONAL		TOTALS
25th Quartile	19.61		19.61		19.19		19.36		74.46
Median	17.30		17.55		17.10		17.63		70.23
75th Quartile	15.13		15.46		15.04		14.68		61.69
Quartile Range	4.48		4.15		4.15		4.69		12.77
Company	Points	Rank	Points	Rank	Points	Rank	Points	Rank	Points
A	20.10	11	18.25	25	18.63	20	14.55	48	71.53
B	18.71	21	17.60	30	15.92	39	17.75	30	69.98
C	14.42	51	15.31	48	16.46	37	12.55	58	58.74
D	20.67	9	18.65	22	17.13	31	21.40	7	77.84
E	16.40	39	18.70	21	21.25	5	17.25	33	73.60

125

Figure 9-4. BBP Portal Worker's Compensation Metric, SYSCO*

■ = 25th quartile

■ = 75th quartile

	DELIVERY EXPENSE, % OF SALES				WAREHOUSE EXPENSE, % OF SALES				WORKER'S COMPENSATION, % OF SALES				SHRINK, % OF SALES				COST PER CASE			
SYSCO Food Service	4.15%		4.13%		2.77%		2.84%		0.22%		0.23%		0.26%		0.30%		3.57		3.48	
Company	Dec-00	Rank	Dec-99	Rank	Dec-00	Rank	Dec-99	Rank	Dec-00	Rank	Dec-99	Rank	Dec-00	Rank	Dec-99	Rank	Dec-00	Rank	Dec-99	Rank
A	4.62%	52	4.33%	39	2.90%	42	2.99%	40	0.20%	38	0.13%	22	0.21%	22	0.29%	35	4.22	55	3.89	
B	4.36%	44	4.40%	41	2.33%	15	2.32%	12	0.11%	18	0.09%	10	0.27%	40	0.28%	30	3.52	28	3.39	

* Numbers and percentages are representative, not actual. Comparisons and trends are accurate.

information on a number of more specific measures that feed into or drive the overall worker's compensation metric. This provides a fine-tuned set of data for understanding what is driving worker's compensation costs. Again, these data are provided over the past two years for all of the business units so that you can determine the specific driver or drivers that should be the focus of attention. See Figure 9-5.

Select Shared Best Practices

The final level of the system is the best practices. Thus far the portal has enabled you to analytically assess the problem areas from a general level down to specific drivers. The next step entails providing solutions to those problem areas. By searching the portal under worker's compensation best practices, you can access several resources. For example, the 5-STAR guidebook, discussed earlier, provides some general best practices in regard to safety. The portal also provides access to the best practices adopted by the top-performing companies.

Seeing Results

This basic model, process, and portal have been used in many ways to improve performance. One of the best examples was with regard to safety performance, as in the previous example. Early in 1998, company leaders thought that increasing safety performance could generate significant cost savings. Consequently, a goal was set of reducing the performance gap between the top 25% and bottom 25% of companies in safety.

Leveraging the communications system, business units were encouraged to focus at least some of their efforts on increasing safety performance by using the BBP Web portal. Top-performing companies provided their best-practices safety information, and bottom-performing

Figure 9-5. BBP Portal Main Factors Driving Worker's Compensation (WC) Costs, SYSCO*

COMPANY	FY2002 MAY YTD WC $ AS % OF JUNE YEAR-TO-DATE SALES	FY2000 MAY YTD WC $ AS % OF JUNE YEAR-TO-DATE SALES	FY2001 ANNUALIZED WC FREQUENCY	FY2002 ANNUALIZED WC FREQUENCY	FY2001 OPEN CLAIMS PER 100 EMPLOYEES	FY2000 OPEN CLAIMS PER 100 EMPLOYEES	FY2001 WC CLAIM REPORTING LAG TIME (DAYS)	FY2000 WC CLAIM REPORTING LAG TIME (DAYS)
A	0.04%	0.06%	5.19	10.4	1.76	1.82	6.47	11.00
B	0.06%	0.07%	10.04	11.16	1.36	2.36	2.57	5.40

*Numbers and percentages are representative, not actual. Comparisons and trends are accurate.

companies both accessed the online information and contacted the top-performing companies for direct information and help. After five years, the overall worker's compensation costs (as a percentage of sales) had been reduced to 0.10% from 0.22%, as a percentage of sales. These numbers may not sound like much, but they represented a significant improvement in performance and an annual cost savings of $36 million (Figure 9-6).

We conclude this chapter with samples of metrics that can be used to help determine the impact of people practices on organizational performance. Figures 9-7 and 9-8 demonstrate some of the innumerable ways that human capital performance can be measured.

Figure 9-6. Significant Financial Improvement with Improved Safety, SYSCO

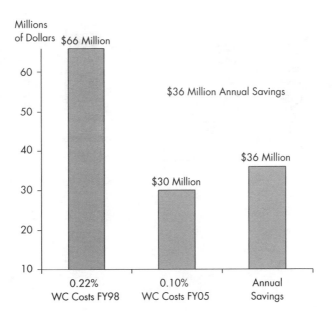

Figure 9-7. Measuring the Impact of Leadership Practices, Orientation, and Rewards, SYSCO*

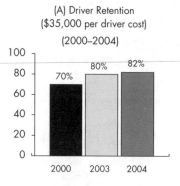

(A) Driver Retention
($35,000 per driver cost)
(2000–2004)

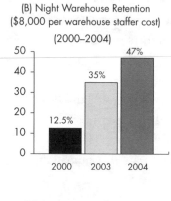

(B) Night Warehouse Retention
($8,000 per warehouse staffer cost)
(2000–2004)

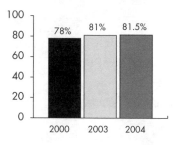

(C) Marketing Associate Retention
($50,000 per marketing associate cost)

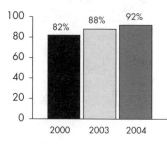

(D) Corporate Headquarters
Retention

*Numbers and percentages are representative, not actual. Comparisons and trends are accurate.

Building Profit through Building People

Figure 9-8. Measuring the Impact of Industry Relations/Diversity Activities, SYSCO*

(A) Corporate—Officers

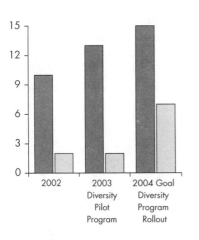

(B) Corporate—Senior Director/
Director Level

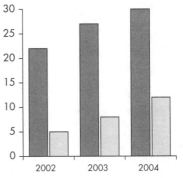

(C) Operating Companies—
President/Executive Vice President

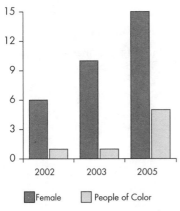

(D) Operating Companies—
Senior Vice President/Vice President Level

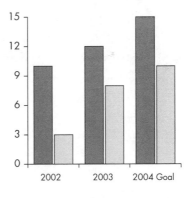

■ Female   ☐ People of Color

*Numbers and percentages are representative, not actual. Comparisons and trends are accurate.

Overview

A dynamic 5-STAR model keeps business leaders focused on performance that matters while encouraging constant innovation to improve it. Building such a model entails providing a common metrics model that can focus attention on the key performance areas; building an information system that makes data available to all interested parties in a way that sparks a desire to continuously improve; and creating a culture that enables users to share best practices and learn from those who have developed them.

RECAP:

1. The 5-STAR model must be flexible to shift with the business conditions.
2. Metrics must be well defined and represent all areas of business performance.
3. A well-integrated information technology system can be a crucial component for utilizing metrics across the business.
4. Motivating associates to continue developing and sharing best practices is essential to long-term success.

CHAPTER 10

A Strategic Summons for Human Resources

Volumes have been written in recent years to redefine the role of the HR professional. Buzzwords like "re-engineering" and "strategic alignment"—phrases often used to describe the revenue-generating parts of the business—are now being applied to HR. It is easy to claim that HR is functioning differently—that the field has moved beyond the "personnel manager" days of the past—but it is much harder to operationalize these new, business-critical behaviors.

As we conclude, we want to briefly review the main principles previously established and remind ourselves of the actions and competencies behind re-engineering and strategic alignment. But we also want to spend some time introducing you to the importance of two new concepts: what the HR function delivers and how the HR function is structured. Both of these concepts are key to adding value and creating competitive advantage for an organization.

Even if you do not work in the HR part of an organization, you likely partner with someone in HR regularly, so we encourage you to examine the principles set forth here and see how they might drive you and your teams to greater success. We also encourage you to remember that the re-engineering, so to speak, of the HR profession is a journey. New tools and techniques are continually being developed. Various companies of all shapes and sizes are experimenting with the ideal way to structure their administrative functions for maximum effectiveness. Do not read this chapter as a definitive road map, but consider it a compass to point you in the best direction.

HR Competencies

We all know that the goal of any company is to create sustained economic value by delivering needed products or services. That value is measured by the company's superiority in long-term return on investment. First and foremost, HR professionals must understand these concepts. They must be adept at articulating how their business operates, knowing each link in the value-profit chain. This knowledge not only builds credibility with line business leaders, but also it ensures that they are able to adapt organizational activities to changing business conditions. HR leaders also need to position themselves as business partners and demonstrate mastery of people issues. For it is people issues that are the critical drivers of competitiveness in any organization.

Dave Ulrich (1996) originally defined four competencies that provide the basic framework for how the HR professional must operate. These are set forth in Figure 10-1.

Ulrich's pyramid clearly defines the behaviors and skills that HR team members need to continually develop and refine. Now, in a new book, *The HR Value Proposition*, Dave Ulrich and Wayne Brockbank continue to build on the importance of the four competencies and provide additional direction concerning the importance of knowing the external business realities and how to create and add value. Mastery of traditional HR functions—such as staffing, development, rewards, and employee relations—is a given. Personal credibility is also a ticket to

Figure 10-1. Key HR Competencies

Reprinted with permission. *Human Resource Champions,* P. 251, David Ulrich: Boston: Harvard Business Press, 1997.

entry in the HR field. What is *new* is the mastery of the business and skill in managing change. Developing these two competencies is crucial in the ever-changing business world of the twenty-first century. Refining and developing the HR competencies are essential to being a strategic partner, but just as important are the two other concepts mentioned above:

- what the HR function delivers; and
- how the HR function is structured.

What HR Delivers

Implicit in strategic HR and in what the HR function delivers is a concept that is of increasing importance: an analytical approach to HR. In contrast to HR professionals' previous passive, order-taking role, an analytical approach requires (a) proactively conceptualizing problems and devising systems-oriented solutions, and (b) having the ability to gather, analyze, interpret, and apply data of all kinds.

Proactively Developing Systems-Oriented Solutions

How often does HR drive the agenda for business discussions versus simply listening to the requests of others? Being proactive requires that HR professionals move from waiting for directions or information from other business leaders to gathering, analyzing, and disseminating the data that are needed.

To be proactive, HR professionals also must be able to conceptualize problems from a systems perspective. This approach means looking at problems and possible solutions with a long-term, corporate wide view, not just a short-term, narrow perspective. Leaders at one company (which, for reasons you'll see, will remain nameless) attempted to improve profits quickly through downsizing the workforce. With the HR function simply taking orders, to save the most money the layoff focused on long-service, highly paid personnel. This strategy successfully reduced costs. However, the laid-off employees were those who generated the highest revenues. In addition, the remaining employees suffered morale problems, decreased enthusiasm, and increased cynicism. The drop in revenue resulted in lower profits, prompting management to downsize further to readjust costs to revenues. Had HR taken a systems approach, there might have been a better long-term result.

We only wish such cases were the exception, rather than the rule. However, too frequently, HR professionals have simply deferred problem-solving to other business leaders. HR professionals must be out front, ahead of the business instead of waiting to hear what the business says. They must identify the issues that the company will confront long before the other business leaders know the issues are coming. Unless and until those in HR can identify potential problem areas ahead of other business leaders and then conceptualize and communicate systemic solutions, the HR function will be relegated to the role of order-taker rather than agenda-setter.

Understanding and Using Data

Being proactive and conceptualizing problems requires an ability to understand and use data that is often lacking among HR professionals. HR metrics seemingly consume more and more attention and effort, yet often with little payoff. This failure says nothing about metrics and everything about those who try to use them. An analytical approach to HR requires that professionals must understand the basic issues of measurement, analysis, and interpretation of data—and also understand that these tools are necessary to implement change in the business environment. Recently, an HR executive mentioned that he wanted to convince his business leaders to double the company's adoption benefit from $5,000 to $10,000. He argued that this benefit would increase retention of those who utilize it. However, he was unable to present any data to support his argument. And his answer suggested that he would not know where to begin to gather the data that might support the argument.

Contrast this with the SYSCO example. As we have shown in this book, data gathering and analysis are the foundations for the market-driven approach to HR. The unique structure, culture, and governance mean that influence stems from data, not from authority. Persuading independent business-unit presidents requires more than slick salesmanship; it requires presenting hard-nosed data that support value propositions and illustrate how to achieve business goals.

Data-gathering and analysis support a market-driven human capital function in two important ways. First, SYSCO HR established a sophisticated and integrated overview of autonomous key metrics.

These include human capital measures as well as financial, operational, customer service, quality, and governance metrics. These metrics link to the overall business strategy and are adjusted annually (or perhaps even quarterly) to reflect changes in the business. The measures tie to the performance management process and drive both individual and organizational goals. Figure 10-2 shows key metrics for the entire organization's effectiveness, as developed and published by the strategic planning group in HR.

Second, some of the HR services provided are optional and can be customized for the operating centers, depending on the unique needs of their customers or their own operations. This flexibility is essential to the market-driven model of service delivery. HR only delivers the services that the lines of business deem necessary to their success.

While SYSCO presents a unique situation, we are confident that the effectiveness of a data-driven approach crosses business boundaries to work for all types of organizations.

Delivering a Human Capital Model

As an example of what HR can deliver when the function is proactive, systems-oriented, and data-driven, let's look at the human capital model used at both Continental and SYSCO. The HR function was differentiated from other important operations by establishing this human capital model and communicating it throughout the companies. This basic model, grounded in business strategy, is illustrated in Figure 10-3.

Reading from the bottom of the pyramid up, you can see that the model is driven by the business strategy and a commitment to operational effectiveness. Having this foundation is absolutely essential to the validity and strength of the overall structure.

The next level up is to use exceptional communication practices to establish a common understanding among all the business constituen-

Figure 10-2. Operational Effectiveness Metrics, SYSCO

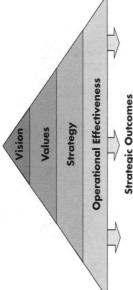

Customer	Financial	Human Capital	Operations	Governance	Supply Chain
Loyal Customers	ROI/EPS	Loyal/ Productive Workforce	Operational Excellence	Sustainability	Cost/ Competitive Advantage
FY03–04	FY03–04	FY03–04	FY03–04	FY03–04	FY03–04
• Service Level • Sales Growth • Market Share	• Operating Expense to Sales • Earnings	• Climate Survey • Productivity • Safety	• Delivery Expense to Sales • Warehouse Expense • Pieces per Trip	• ROE • Audit Scores	• Transportation Savings • Total Cost Reduction • Cost of Goods

Vision
Values
Strategy
Operational Effectiveness

Strategic Outcomes

139

Figure 10-3. The Seven C's Human Capital Model

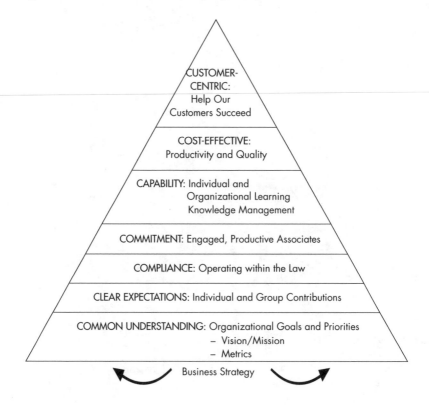

cies regarding goals, priorities, mission, vision, metrics, and what the business is trying to do. We have found that it is impossible to emphasize your company's core vision and mission too frequently. These concepts need to be fully embraced by your people.

Next is setting clear expectations. Employees must understand what is expected of them so that they can be most productive. They have to have a clear line-of-sight to how they can have an impact on business effectiveness, as well as what they need to do to have such an impact. This, of course, becomes the driver for your company's performance management process.

Building Profit through Building People

Moving up the model, the next sections concern compliance, commitment, and capability. First, a company must operate within the law and often go beyond the law to meet societal expectations. Second, the company must hire, develop, and retain engaged, productive employees. While organizations and analysts tend to talk more and more about the "new deal" and the "free agent" career, competitive advantage stems only from building an organization full of missionaries who believe in its cause, rather than mercenaries who believe only in a paycheck. Finally, in a world filled with rapid and unpredictable change, the company must establish an ongoing process for individual and organizational learning and knowledge management. The skills of the workforce today will barely overlap with those required in 10 years, and maybe even in 5 years, so companies must develop a process for continual learning.

Finally, at the tip of the pyramid are a relentless focus on cost effectiveness through productivity and quality and a commitment to being a customer-centric organization. At the end of the day, organizations should be about helping customers be successful. Note that cost effectiveness does not equate with cost reduction. Customers demand value and are often willing to pay a higher price for what they perceive will provide higher value.

How HR Is Structured

To effectively implement such a human capital model, the HR function must be optimally structured. First, the HR organization should be market-driven, as discussed above. Second, it must be structured to fulfill its traditional role while working toward a second, innovative role as a strategic business partner.

Many HR organizations and HR professionals attempt to be all things to all people—to expand their "generalist" roles when the organization needs more narrow and expert support from the HR function. Our position is that this generalist approach cannot be done effectively and should not be done. We recommend that in order to help differentiate the organization and provide unique value to its customers, the HR structure should consist both of *traditional centers of expertise* (staffing, rewards, employee relations, knowledge management, strategy, and organization development) and *transformational centers of expertise* that optimize the value that can be created by investing in and leveraging of human capital in that organization. Figure 10-4 shows how these two centers of expertise are integral to a human capital structure.

Figure 10-4. Human Capital Structure, SYSCO

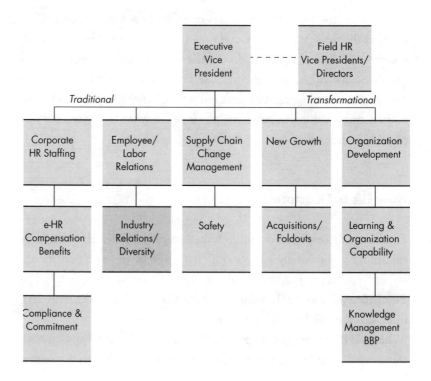

Building Profit through Building People

As you optimize your HR organizational structure and establish appropriate metrics, you must be sure to perform the activities necessary to help transform the entire organization in keeping with the mantra, "It's all about people." The list of activities includes strategic planning, knowledge management, acquisition and integration of talent, and so forth. It is important to remember that to enhance HR's ability to make a bottom-line impact on the organization, HR professionals must first build and maintain personal credibility. In addition, HR professionals cannot be effective unless they are passionate about making the lives of employees more productive and purposeful and unless they are committed to becoming strategic business partners. HR team members can have significant, strategic impact when they

- are smart about the business;
- know what is expected of them;
- determine how to influence most effectively;
- identify what is right and practical; and
- stand for what is right, not necessarily popular.

By applying these principles and practices, we believe that HR professionals can be key players in any organization and move well beyond the traditional administrative role typically assigned to their profession. To get there though, takes commitment, guts, and gumption. Many business leaders are accustomed to thinking of HR as the "personnel function." It takes willingness on both sides to build an effective partnership that influences the business and helps harness the human capital of the organization to achieve sustained business success.

Next Steps

What are some practical steps you can use at this point? You might be thinking that your organization is far, far away from adopting a new organizational structure or looking at HR through a new set of lenses. But many have gone before you, and they constantly modify their approaches and plans of attack to achieve their goals of higher functioning. Here are a few specific ideas.

If you have not perused the material in the "Resources" section at the back of this book, we encourage you to do so and to set some personal goals.

If you have not joined the Society for Human Resource Management, we encourage you to do so and avail yourself of the excellent resources it offers for HR process and structural re-engineering. Share with line management the success stories of companies that have realigned their HR functions to be more connected to the business and as a result have seen measurable performance improvement related to the company's strategy.

If your HR team members are not attending line management meetings, help get them in the door. It is imperative that HR professionals be part of these discussions in order to understand the nuances of the business and establish credibility. HR staff should also consider going on customer calls or sitting in on operational reviews to get a firsthand look at business challenges. Developing facilitation skills and becoming the go-to person when a management team needs some "objective, outside help" is another way to get in front of the business and insert yourself into the strategic planning process.

To build financial savvy, consider attending training classes to build understanding of the fundamentals of business. Many individuals enter the HR field with a non-business-related degree and may have only limited exposure to the workings of a profit-and-loss sheet or a business plan. Sitting in on your own organization's sales training may be another way to build business acumen while also gaining visibility among key business leaders.

These are just a few tactical ideas to help you achieve your goals of becoming a more strategic business partner, establishing a market-driven set of deliverables, and structuring HR to be optimally aligned to the business.

We conclude by encouraging you to do a bit of meditation. There appears to be a movement or trend toward the HR function being a trustee of the organization's social system. In essence, the role of HR is not only focused on human capital but on social capital—and on how collaboratively and effectively the organization works. In effect, HR is the trustee of the right people in the right jobs, the code of conduct, and the important link between performance and compensation.

Consider carefully, then, not only the strengths and weaknesses of your HR team today but also the structure, quality, and quantity of service delivery from the team in the future. Determine both short-term and long-term strategies to propel you to a new level of functional expertise and organizational impact. Only then will it be possible to see how satisfied people and effective processes can, in fact, drive organizations to sustained peak performance and growth.

After all, it's all about people.

APPENDIX A

Customer Satisfaction Survey, SYSCO

Food establishment name: _____

Name of person
responding to survey: _____

Title: _____

Date: _____

SYSCO operating company (company you buy from):

_____

Based on your recent experience during the past 2–3 months, please provide us with your candid assessment. Your input will help us do a better job of serving you. Thank you for your business and for taking time to respond to this survey.

	Completely Agree	Agree	Neutral	Disagree	Completely Disagree
1. SYSCO provides support and services that help my business succeed.	❏	❏	❏	❏	❏

	Completely Satisfied	Satisfied	Neutral	Dissatisfied	Completely Dissatisfied
2. Based upon your recent experience during the past 2–3 months, on an overall basis how satisfied are you with SYSCO?	❏	❏	❏	❏	❏
3. With regard to receiving every item you ordered, how satisfied are you with SYSCO?	❏	❏	❏	❏	❏
4. With regard to on-time delivery, how satisfied are you with SYSCO?	❏	❏	❏	❏	❏
5. How satisfied are you with the accuracy of invoices from SYSCO?	❏	❏	❏	❏	❏
6. How satisfied are you with the safety and wholesomeness of the products you buy from SYSCO?	❏	❏	❏	❏	❏
7. How satisfied are you with the fairness and competitiveness of SYSCO's prices?	❏	❏	❏	❏	❏

8. How satisfied are you with the condition of products delivered by SYSCO (relative to damage)?

9. How satisfied are you with the variety of products offered by SYSCO?

10. How satisfied are you with the ease and convenience of ordering from SYSCO?

11. How satisfied are you overall with the helpfulness of your SYSCO Marketing Associate?

12. How satisfied are you with your SYSCO Marketing Associate as a:

   a. Business Partner—knowing your operation and helping you effectively grow/manage your business?

   b. Customer Service Source—assisting you in getting what you need?

   c. Menu Analysis and Planning—evaluating and assisting with your menu requirements?

   d. Product Information Specialist—providing sources of product expertise?

   e. Problem Solver—providing you with appropriate business solutions?

13. How satisfied are you overall with the helpfulness of your:

   a. SYSCO Customer Service Rep?

   b. SYSCO Delivery Associate?

14. When a problem occurs, how satisfied are you with SYSCO's ability to respond and quickly resolve the problem?

❏   ❏   ❏   ❏   ❏

15. Of the services below, please check off the five you consider to be the most important priorities for you:
❏ Complete delivery of every item ordered
❏ On-time delivery
❏ Invoice accuracy
❏ Provide support and services beyond food that help my business succeed
❏ Fair, competitive price
❏ Receiving product undamaged
❏ Wide variety of products
❏ Ease and convenience of ordering
❏ Marketing Associate/Sales Representative knowledge
❏ Customer Service Representative knowledge
❏ Delivery Associate/Driver helpfulness
❏ Ability to respond and quickly resolve problems

16. During the past 2–3 months, approximately what percentage of your total food purchases did you buy from SYSCO?
❏ 0–20%   ❏ 20–40%   ❏ 40–60%   ❏ 60–80%   ❏ 80–100%

17. In your view, do you use a foodservice distributor who out-performs SYSCO?
❏ Yes   Name of distributor _____
❏ No

18. If you answered yes to question 17, in your opinion what does the other distributor do better than SYSCO?

_____

_____

_____

Thank you for your assistance!
Please return your completed survey in the enclosed postage-paid envelope. If you have any questions, please call toll-free: _____ .

Cover Letter for the Work-Climate Improvement Survey, SYSCO

MEMORANDUM

TO:	SYSCO Associates
FROM:	President and COO
DATE:	
RE:	Associate Work Climate Survey

As part of our commitment to being a STAR Employer, I am asking that all associates complete the Work Climate Survey. The last time we administered the Work Climate Survey we received feedback from over 80% of the corporate associates.

We value the comments and suggestions you made through the survey. As a dirct result of your feedback on previous surveys, please find a sample of the office-wide changes we have made:

- Monthly President Roundtable meetings
- Guaranteed match on eligible 401(k) contributions
- Year-round business casual dress on Fridays and business casual dress on Mondays during the summer months
- Annual company Incentive Bonus to all associates

In addition to these improvements, as a result of the survey many departments have made enhancements to the way that they share information, which improves the way that we conduct business.

Later today, you will receive an e-mail from Cornell University with instructions on how to access the survey. You will have until August 1, 2004 to complete the survey. As in the past, Cornell will analyze the information to ensure confidentiality of all responses.

Cornell will return to us a summary of our overall results. Additionally, by mid-October each officer will receive a summary of the feedback from the associates on his/her team. We will use the results of the survey to reflect on our areas of strength and identify areas in which we will continue to strive for improvements.

I appreciate your comments and dedication to SYSCO. We look forward to hearing your thoughts and suggestions on how SYSCO can continue to be the STAR employer in Houston. As always, we will assess the changes we can make to remain fair in our offerings to associates, while maintaining a competitive cost structure as we serve our customers. If you have any questions regarding the survey, please contact the HR Director.

Work-Climate Improvement Survey, SYSCO

We appreciate your participation in this study to determine ways we can continue to improve our workplace.

Your participation is extremely important because it is a good way to assess what management practices work best. SYSCO has joined with Cornell University in sponsoring this associate satisfaction study. Cornell University has aided various industries by providing an objective perspective on how associates feel about their workplace. Completed surveys will be mailed directly to Cornell University. Please take your time when completing the survey. This survey will take about 30 minutes to complete.

Your answers are strictly confidential.

You are part of a group that can positively impact our workplace. As an associate, your satisfaction is of critical importance to SYSCO. That's why we need you to complete the attached questionnaire and place it in the confidential envelope.

We greatly appreciate your feedback and insights, and we look forward to sharing the findings with you in the near future.

Please use blue or black ink to complete the survey.

Thank you for your cooperation.

PART I. DEMOGRAPHIC INFORMATION

My job is (Please select only one):

- ❑ Administration-Accounting/Finance
- ❑ Administrative
- ❑ Administrative-Other
- ❑ Marketing
- ❑ Marketing Associate
- ❑ Customer Service
- ❑ Fleet Maintenance/Facilities
- ❑ Driver

- ❑ Merchandising
- ❑ Night Warehouse
- ❑ Day Warehouse
- ❑ Supervisor-Administrative
- ❑ Supervisor-Operations
- ❑ Supervisor-Sales
- ❑ Other-Operations
- ❑ Other

My Operating Company is: _____ Location: _____

Building Profit through Building People

PART II. JOB SATISFACTION

Section A: Leadership Support

Please choose only one response for each question.

	Strongly Disagree	Disagree	Neither Agree nor Disagree	Agree	Strongly Agree
A1. I know what is expected of me at work.	❏	❏	❏	❏	❏
A2. I have a reasonable workload to do my job well.	❏	❏	❏	❏	❏
A3. At work, I have the opportunity to put my skills to good use.	❏	❏	❏	❏	❏
A4. I have an opportunity to influence decisions that directly impact my work.	❏	❏	❏	❏	❏
A5. I am informed whenever decisions are to be made that affect my job.	❏	❏	❏	❏	❏
A6. I know the business goals of the company.	❏	❏	❏	❏	❏
A7. Communication from upper management (President, Executive Vice President, etc.) is open and honest.	❏	❏	❏	❏	❏
A8. Upper management demonstrates their commitment to build a diverse workforce.	❏	❏	❏	❏	❏
A9. Upper management (President, Executive Vice President, etc.) spends time talking with associates about our business direction.	❏	❏	❏	❏	❏

Section B: Strengthen Front-line Supervisor

Please choose only one response for each question.

	Strongly Disagree	Disagree	Neither Agree nor Disagree	Agree	Strongly Agree
B1. My supervisor treats me with dignity and respect.	❑	❑	❑	❑	❑
B2. My supervisor cares about me as a person.	❑	❑	❑	❑	❑
B3. I receive timely, specific, fair, and ongoing feedback.	❑	❑	❑	❑	❑
B4. My supervisor encourages my involvement in solving a problem or improving a situation.	❑	❑	❑	❑	❑
B5. My supervisor helps me whenever I ask for help.	❑	❑	❑	❑	❑
B6. My supervisor and I review my top goals and discuss how they contribute to the company's success.	❑	❑	❑	❑	❑
B7. When I make a mistake, my supervisor and I share ideas on what I could have done differently.	❑	❑	❑	❑	❑
B8. I have received constructive feedback on my performance within the last 6 months.	❑	❑	❑	❑	❑
B9. My supervisor encourages my career development.	❑	❑	❑	❑	❑
B10. My supervisor does his/her best to make SYSCO a good place to work.	❑	❑	❑	❑	❑
B11. My supervisor is quite competent in doing his/her job.	❑	❑	❑	❑	❑
B12. My supervisor removes obstacles so I can do my job better.	❑	❑	❑	❑	❑

Section C: Quality of Life

Please choose only one response for each question.

	Strongly Disagree	Disagree	Neither Agree nor Disagree	Agree	Strongly Agree
C1. I trust what the company tells me.	☐	☐	☐	☐	☐
C2. I know whom to call to get help solving problems.	☐	☐	☐	☐	☐
C3. I feel our rules and procedures do not prevent me from doing a good job.	☐	☐	☐	☐	☐
C4. Different departments of our company work together to get the job done.	☐	☐	☐	☐	☐
C5. I have the proper materials and equipment I need to do my job right.	☐	☐	☐	☐	☐
C6. I feel my work environment is safe.	☐	☐	☐	☐	☐
C7. I like the people I work with.	☐	☐	☐	☐	☐
C8. This is a good place to work.	☐	☐	☐	☐	☐
C9. My co-workers and I take the initiative to solve workplace problems together.	☐	☐	☐	☐	☐
C10. I have received sufficient training to do my job effectively.	☐	☐	☐	☐	☐
C11. I have had opportunities to learn new things at work within the past year.	☐	☐	☐	☐	☐
C12. I am given opportunities to learn and develop new skills for future advancement.	☐	☐	☐	☐	☐

Section C: Quality of Life, continued

	Strongly Disagree	Disagree	Neither Agree nor Disagree	Agree	Strongly Agree
C13. Compared to other companies in my area, I feel SYSCO is accommodating to my work and family balance.	❏	❏	❏	❏	❏
C14. I feel SYSCO is generally responsive to my work and personal concerns.	❏	❏	❏	❏	❏
C15. My organization values the contributions of employees regardless of race, gender, or ethnic background.	❏	❏	❏	❏	❏
C16. My organization has a culture that fosters new ideas from employees regardless of race, gender, or ethnic background.	❏	❏	❏	❏	❏

Building Profit through Building People

Section D: Customer Focus

Please choose only one response for each question.

	Strongly Disagree	Disagree	Neither Agree nor Disagree	Agree	Strongly Agree
D1. I am committed to doing high-quality work and providing quality service.	❑	❑	❑	❑	❑
D2. I am able to make decisions required to meet or exceed customer requirements.	❑	❑	❑	❑	❑
D3. My efforts to do a good job for customers are not blocked by red tape.	❑	❑	❑	❑	❑
D4. I work constantly to improve our products and services.	❑	❑	❑	❑	❑
D5. The products we offer our customers are the best available.	❑	❑	❑	❑	❑
D6. I know what is important to our customers.	❑	❑	❑	❑	❑

Section E: Rewards

Please choose only one response for each question.

	Strongly Disagree	Disagree	Neither Agree nor Disagree	Agree	Strongly Agree
E1. I feel I am being paid a fair amount for the work I do.	❑	❑	❑	❑	❑
E2. My pay is the same or better than that of other companies in our market.	❑	❑	❑	❑	❑
E3. My benefits are the same or better than those of other companies in our market.	❑	❑	❑	❑	❑
E4. Doing my job well leads to monetary rewards.	❑	❑	❑	❑	❑
E5. Doing my job well leads to recognition and respect from those I work with.	❑	❑	❑	❑	❑
E6. My supervisor seeks opportunities to provide me with positive feedback on a job well done.	❑	❑	❑	❑	❑
E7. Decisions made about promotions or job changes within this organization are fair.	❑	❑	❑	❑	❑

Building Profit through Building People

Section F: Inclusion through Engagement and Diversity

Please choose only one response for each question.

	Strongly Disagree	Disagree	Neither Agree nor Disagree	Agree	Strongly Agree
F1. I am willing to work harder to help this company succeed.	❑	❑	❑	❑	❑
F2. I am proud to work for SYSCO.	❑	❑	❑	❑	❑
F3. I feel a strong sense of belonging to this organization.	❑	❑	❑	❑	❑
F4. I feel a diverse workforce contributes to SYSCO's success.	❑	❑	❑	❑	❑
F5. I am comfortable building relationships with peers or customers who are different from me.	❑	❑	❑	❑	❑
F6. I would refer a friend to come work at SYSCO.	❑	❑	❑	❑	❑
F7. I provide constructive suggestions about how my department can improve its effectiveness.	❑	❑	❑	❑	❑
F8. I would turn down a job with more pay in order to stay with SYSCO.	❑	❑	❑	❑	❑
F9. I plan to spend my career at SYSCO.	❑	❑	❑	❑	❑
F10. I intend to stay at SYSCO for at least the next 12 months.	❑	❑	❑	❑	❑
F11. Overall, I am satisfied working at SYSCO.	❑	❑	❑	❑	❑

Section G: Work Values

G1. The one thing that I like best about SYSCO is: (Please write within the box only.)

G2. The one thing I would like to change about SYSCO is: (Please write within the box only.)

Please feel free to provide any further comments below: (Please write within the box only.)

Building Profit through Building People

The remaining questions are to be used by Cornell University for research purposes only. Please answer these questions to the best of your ability.

Section H: Discretionary Behavior

Please choose only one response for each question.

	Strongly Disagree	Disagree	Neither Agree nor Disagree	Agree	Strongly Agree
H1. For issues that may have serious consequences, I express my opinions honestly even when others may disagree.	❑	❑	❑	❑	❑
H2. I touch base with my co-workers before initiating actions that might affect them.	❑	❑	❑	❑	❑
H3. I encourage others to try new and effective ways of doing their job.	❑	❑	❑	❑	❑
H4. I help others who have large amounts of work.	❑	❑	❑	❑	❑
H5. I willingly share my expertise with my co-workers.	❑	❑	❑	❑	❑
H6. I do not plan to look for a job outside of this company in the next 6 months.	❑	❑	❑	❑	❑

PART III. MANAGEMENT PRACTICES

In the following sections, please answer the questions about management practices based on how you think your co-workers in your department would respond. When you answer the questions, think about the experiences of your co-workers as well as your own experiences with the company. Please take your time and think about your entire department when answering the questions.

Please choose only one response for each question.

		Yes	No	I Don't Know
1.	Applicants for this job take formal tests (paper and pencil or work sample) before being hired.	☐	☐	☐
2.	Applicants for this job undergo structured interviews (job related questions, same questions asked for all applicants) before being hired.	☐	☐	☐
3.	Associates in this job are involved in formal participation processes such as quality improvement groups, problem solving groups, or roundtable discussions.	☐	☐	☐
4.	Associates in this job have a reasonable and fair complaint process.	☐	☐	☐
5.	Associates in this job have the opportunity to earn group bonuses for productivity, performance, or other group performance outcomes.	☐	☐	☐
6.	Applicants for this job have the opportunity to earn individual bonuses (or commissions) for productivity, performance, or other individual performance outcomes.	☐	☐	☐
7.	At least once a year associates in this job receive a formal evaluation of their performance.	☐	☐	☐
8.	Associates in this job regularly receive formal communication regarding company goals and objectives.	☐	☐	☐
9.	In the last 4 months, the company has made a change in how work is completed in my department based on the suggestion(s) of an associate or group of associates.	☐	☐	☐
10.	Pay raises for associates in this job are based on job performance.	☐	☐	☐

Building Profit through Building People

PART III. MANAGEMENT PRACTICES, continued

11. Qualified associates in this job have the opportunity to be promoted to positions of greater pay and/or responsibility within the company.

12. Associates in this job are allowed to make important work related decisions such as how the work is done or implement new ideas.

	Strongly Disagree	Disagree	Neither Agree nor Disagree	Agree	Strongly Agree
11.			❑	❑	❑
12.			❑	❑	❑
13. The company hires only the very best people for this job.			❑	❑	❑
14. Total pay for this job is the highest for this type of work in the area.			❑	❑	❑

Please choose only one response.

15. On average, how many hours of formal training do associates in this job receive each year?

❑ 0–5 hours   ❑ 6–10 hours   ❑ 11–15 hours   ❑ 16–20 hours

❑ 21–25 hours   ❑ 26–30 hours   ❑ 31–35 hours   ❑ 35+ hours

The information provided below will be kept completely confidential and will be used only by Cornell University.

Please choose only one response for each question, where applicable.

My age is:

❏ Under 21 ❏ 21–29 years ❏ 30–39 years ❏ 40–49 years ❏ 50 or over

My gender is:

❏ Male ❏ Female

(Optional) My race/ethnic group is:

❏ White ❏ Black ❏ Hispanic ❏ Asian or Pacific Islander ❏ American Indian or Alaskan Native

My educational background is:

❏ Some high school ❏ Two-year degree ❏ High School degree or equivalent ❏ Bachelor's degree ❏ Some college

❏ Other

I have worked at my current job for:

❏ <6 months ❏ 6 months–1 year ❏ 1–2 years ❏ 2–5 years ❏ 5–10 years

❏ 10+ years

My job title/function is:

How many days did you miss from work in the last 12 months (excluding vacation)? _____ days

Thank you for your participation!

Building Profit through Building People

Lesson Outline from Strengthening the Front-line Supervisor Program, SYSCO

Desired Results of the Program

1. Improve customer focus and operations service level.
2. Improve associate retention.
3. Increase productivity.
4. Reduce and control inventory shrink.
5. Reinforce and support the SYSCOSafe program.

Achieve Results through Focus Areas

1. Always keep the customer in sight.
2. Provide career development opportunities.
3. Identify and clarify the role and responsibilities of the operations supervisors.
4. Develop a team of *all* operations supervisors, not just by department.
5. Identify and provide tools and training to support the success of supervisors.
6. Train and educate supervisors in all areas of operations.
7. Improve associate relations.
8. Align the incentive program with desired results.

Program Recommended Guidelines

1. *Vice President of Operations/Directors*
   - Reach agreement on defined job description and daily routine.
   - Implement monthly individual goal-setting and performance reviews.
   - Implement an attainable effective supervisor incentive program to be reviewed weekly and paid monthly or quarterly.

- Identify priority focus and goal areas.
- Establish one-hour weekly training sessions for supervisors to accommodate their schedules.
- Modify training material to your company's needs and issues.
- Identify and execute individual and group initiatives to improve by category.
- Install television monitors to communicate information to employees through PowerPoint presentations.

2. *Supervisors*
   - Execute job description and daily routine job functions.
   - Assist in identifying and removing barriers that prevent supervisors from doing their job.
   - Assist in monthly goal setting/performance measurement areas.
   - Participate in the assigned areas of other programs, for example, hiring policy and new-hire training.
   - Participate in weekly training sessions.

Training Overview by Topic

1. *Defined Job Descriptions*
   - Clarify the role and responsibilities of a supervisor.
   - Clarify activities and measurements.
   - Ensure focus on the measurement areas.
   - Identify and remove obstacles that prevent supervisors from doing their jobs.
   - Identify individual career goals with SYSCO.

2. *Monthly Goal Setting and Performance Reviews*
   - Ensure focus on goals, activities, and measurement areas.
   - Provide structured, timely feedback on performance.
   - Identify training and development needs.

3. *Customer Focus and Operations Service Level*
   - Understand and review the numbers.
   - Understand the effects errors have on the company.
   - Identify, by category, reasons for errors.
   - Identify roles and responsibilities to improve service level by category.
   - Develop and implement initiatives to improve customer service.

4. *Improvement of Employee Retention*
   - Understand the cost and effects associated with turnover.
   - Identify reasons for turnover.

Building Profit through Building People

- Understand the role a supervisor plays in retention.
- Develop and implement initiatives to improve retention.

5. *Increasing Productivity (Cases per Man Hour)*
   - Understand the numbers.
   - Identify reasons for unproductive time.
   - Identify activities and actions to improve efficiency or productivity by department.
   - Review the numbers (actual versus planned) and this year's goals.
   - Develop and implement initiatives to improve productivity and achieve goals.

6. *The SYSCOSafe Program*
   - Review the SYSCO*Safe* program from the supervisor handbook.

7. *Policies and Procedures*
   - Review policies and procedures.
   - Review informational resources available (associate handbook, manuals, and so forth).
   - Identify ways to handle employees' questions.
   - Manage consistently.
   - Review the importance of detailed documentation.
   - Understand legal considerations in employment.

8. *Associate/Labor Relations*
   - Describe the company's position on third-party intervention or mediation.
   - Identify important signs of associate dissatisfaction (what to look for and what to do).
   - Identify factors that drive associate satisfaction.
   - Ways to achieve associate satisfaction.

9. *Employee/Labor Relations (Union Company Considerations)*
   - Know what is in the contract.
   - Understand how to administer labor contracts.

Interpersonal Supervisory Skills Training
1. Build trust and improve associate morale.
2. Communicate clearly and listen actively.
3. Know how to manage conflict.
4. Act in a coaching role and offer feedback.
5. Plan and get organized.
6. Attain proficiency in decision-making.

Some High-Impact Practices and Programs, SYSCO

Many supporting materials for these programs are on the SHRM Web site at www.shrm.org/books/buildingprofit/tools. Programs with supporting materials on the Web are marked with an asterisk (*), and the titles of the materials are given in parentheses at the end of the description.

Other supporting materials are included in this book. Programs with supporting materials in this book are marked with a double asterisk (**), and the locations of the materials are given in parentheses at the end of the description.

5-STAR Actions for Leadership Support

Coaching and Maximizing Performance (CMP): Execute CMP plan. Ensure that associates know what to achieve and how to go about achieving the goal. By setting clear goals that are aligned with your company's overall goals, everyone understands the business better and how their contribution makes a difference.

President Round Tables: Conduct monthly, scheduled, one-hour President Round Tables with 12-15 randomly selected associates. The agenda should include explanation of goals and performance, discussion of barriers and how to remove them, time for associates to share ideas, concerns and problems, discussion of work climate survey/feedback, and highlights of why this remains a great place to work. Ensure that you have diverse representation from all departments and job groups. Invite the selected associates with a letter from the president.

5-STAR Actions for Leadership Support, continued

Monthly Senior Management Meetings: Conduct monthly meetings with senior management to discuss supervisory and associates' issues and brainstorm solutions. Discuss operational issues, work climate issues, supervisor strengths and weaknesses, morale and connectedness of associates, and any diversity initiatives or issues. Determine action steps that need to be taken and timeline for completion. Review the progress that is made on action items and on work climate survey issues.

Annual State-of-the-Company Address: Annually, have the president hold State-of-the-Company meetings for all associates. During the meetings, recap the prior year's performance (corporation-wide for individual operating company), enlighten associates on future goals and plans, reinforce great reasons to work here, and address any issues or questions. Be sensitive to the different job shifts and job groups that may not be easily accessible. You will need to conduct these meetings on every shift.

Executive Team Presence or Management by Walking Around (MBWA): Increase executive team presence around associate work and break areas. Schedule a time each week for the president or a member of the upper management team to visit various work areas. Get to know associates by name. Have upper management stop in break room and eat lunch with associates on an informal basis. Be sensitive to different shifts and job groups that may not be easily accessible. Notice the work environment: observe how associates are treating their workspace, break areas, bathrooms, and customer areas. Be sure to look at the equipment associates use. Are the supervisors ensuring that associates have adequate work equipment and a safe environment? Stagger hours of management team and serve meals to associates on off hours. Remember to thank the associates for their efforts on behalf of the company.

5-STAR Actions to Strengthen the Front-Line Supervisor

*Strengthening the Front-Line Supervisors (SFLS) Training Program: Utilize the SFLS program to ensure that the right people are in supervisor positions, supervisors are clear on their goals, monthly meetings between supervisors and managers occur, incentive systems are structured to ensure supervisors meet their accountabilities, and training occurs so supervisors understand the numbers that they are accountable for and how to impact them. *(Web site: SFLS Program Manual)*

*Monthly Supervisory Meetings: Conduct monthly supervisors meetings. Allow supervisors to discuss performance, pulse of associates, solve issues, determine communication plan, and track results and progress. In addition, the supervisors or the STAR coordinator can prepare minutes of meetings with issues and potential solutions to be reviewed at monthly senior management meetings. These meetings can serve as a forum to discuss areas of interest to front-line supervisors, including benefit plans, retention, staffing, preventive maintenance, overtime, routing, loads, and other important topics. *(Web site: Front-Line Supervisor Development Program SYSCO S.T.E.P. Operations Workbook)*

5-STAR Actions to Strengthen the Front-Line Supervisor, continued

Training Resources: Provide leadership training on how to be a successful supervisor. Training topics may include general leadership skills, conflict resolution, sensitivity training, and improving communication. Also train supervisors on company policies and procedures. Create individual development plan for each front-line supervisor and utilize these resources to assist in their skill development. Resources available include the training library on the intranet, online training classes and resources, and regional training opportunities for new supervisors.

CMP: Execute CMP plan effectively with front-line supervisors to improve their performance. Recommend that middle managers schedule monthly one-on-one meetings with direct reports to discuss their department's performance and individual job performance, and to assess the obstacles that may be preventing them or their associates from performing to the best of their ability. Reward success.

***Coaching to Associates:** Provide the worksheet on work climate survey items and key actions to improve results to front-line supervisors. They can use this tool to assist in performance management of their direct reports. Focus on what needs to get done (goals) as well as how it gets done (skills and behaviors). This worksheet and coaching discussion can help maximize performance based on both manager and associate involvement through two-way communication. Ensure that your supervisors assist associates in removing barriers to improve performance. After these coaching conversations, front-line supervisors also will understand better how they can improve the workplace by implementing suggestions from their associates. *(Figure 6-3)*

**Feedback to Employees:* Ensure the feedback is given from front-line supervisors to your associates. It is important to provide associates with honest feedback in addition to providing them with ideas and suggestions for improvement. Use these meetings as an opportunity to discuss individual associate development and career goals. It is important to give positive reinforcement to associates for a job well done because it encourages the employee to continue to do more of the same. Most employees are motivated by recognition, and others will work to be recognized. Provide feedback and include information about the situation (explain the circumstance), action (what was said or done), and the result (the outcome). *(Web site: Metrics Worksheet)*

5-STAR Actions to Impact Quality of Life

**SYSCOSafe:* Provide supervisors with a SYSCO*Safe* Supervisor Guide to help them make their day-to-day decisions in the areas of SYSCOSafe. Ensure that program is utilized to show preferred work methods, conduct root-cause accident investigations, train associates on safety topics, train new associates on safe work methods, conduct safety committee meetings and handle employee issues appropriately. *(Web site: SYSCOSafe PowerPoint presentation)*

5-STAR Actions to Impact Quality of Life, continued

Ethics Hotline: Promote your company's open-door philosophy, ethics hotline, and employee assistance program by using payroll inserts, posters, and other means of communication. Solicit feedback from associates by conducting regular focus groups, providing associate suggestion boxes, or by having a representative accessible to all associates who can assist with any questions/concerns. Be sure to accommodate all shifts. Watch for trends in the feedback or calls/contacts made to the ethics hotline.

All-Purpose Leave: Implement an all-purpose leave program that combines vacation, sick, personal, and holiday time off to provide greater flexibility and better work/life balance for employees. Creating an all-purpose leave or paid time off (PTO) bank can have advantages and disadvantages. Advantages are: associate flexibility and better work/life balance, effective absence control, consistent administration of time off, reduction of staffing problems as a result of unscheduled time off (increases morale of associates), and promotion of associate responsibility. Associates will perform their best when allowed the flexibility to take time away from work to run errands, visit the doctor, meet parental commitments, take care of personal business, observe non-company holidays, and accommodate unexpected illness. However, employees sometimes perceive that with a PTO bank that they will have less time off than under their old plans. In addition, some associates will come to work even though they should stay home, and those associates who are frequently ill may feel punished. It is important to understand these potential disadvantages prior to the change to a PTO bank. It is also important when determining a PTO bank that you decide what leave is included in the PTO bank (typically bereavement, jury duty, and military leave is not included), how time off will accrue, what happens to unused time off at end of year, what happens when an employee has used all of his or her leave, what holidays are included in PTO bank, and how will time off be tracked effectively.

*SYSCO S.T.E.P. Program: Encourage the development of our associates by allowing them to self-select for supervisory positions. By utilizing the System to Entry-level Promotion (S.T.E.P.) program, future front-line supervisors get a realistic picture of the position and can determine whether it is appropriate for him/her. In addition, by requiring people to post positions internally, SYSCO allows self-nomination. *(Web site: Front-Line Supervisor Development Program SYSCO S.T.E.P. Operations Workbook)*

*One-on-One Meetings: Conduct conversations with individual associates to understand concerns and important drivers of employee satisfaction. Take notes to share at supervisory and senior management meetings to elicit action on key items. Ensure that different groups of employees are selected for individual meetings to get ideas from a broad representation across the organization.

Building Profit through Building People

Family Gatherings: Hold events that include the employees' families. Include family in special holiday events and promotional celebrations. Recognize holidays and special ethnic and cultural events. Hold graduation ceremonies when associates reach important training milestones. Allow employees to bring children to work occasionally to see work environment and explain to them what we do.

5-STAR Actions to Impact Rewards

***ABC Program for Delivery Associates:** Consider implementing activity-based compensation (ABC) systems for delivery associates at your company. ABC allows drivers to be compensated on activities performed instead of hours worked, and the ABC pay systems are based on paying the driver for certain activities that are performed in the scope of delivering product to our customers. Implementing ABC can be a WIN-WIN-WIN for our customers (improved service), drivers (higher pay and quality of life), and the company (greater efficiencies for boosting sales and gaining new customers). *(Web site: ABC PowerPoint slide presentation)*

Competitive Wage Survey: Research current market wage data and evaluate associate wages. Is your company paying at the 50th percentile in your market? Are wages competitive? Refer to compensation surveys conducted by local Chambers of Commerce or other organizations (Society for Human Resources Management (SHRM) www.shrm.org or World at Work www.worldatwork.org) and industry-specific salary surveys. Other HR professionals within the company are another viable resource.

***Benefits Statements:** Educate associates on their current benefits and the value of those benefits. Create a brochure that explains the "hidden paycheck." Cost out your company's contribution to associate fringe benefits. Associates will be surprised at how much additional money the company spends on their behalf. Educate associates on all the great benefits your company provides. If you would like to prepare this material for your associates, there are several software programs available that can assist you in creating the individualized statements. *(Web site: Personalized Benefits Statement)*

Internal Recognition: Recognition is a powerful tool, and when managers/supervisors acknowledge associates for outstanding attitudes and actions, the correct behaviors are reinforced. Develop associate recognition programs that motivate employees to perform (e.g., Associate of Month, Internal CARES program). When creating a program, be creative and get input from associates. Ideas include special parking space, a car wash by a manager or executive, recognition section in the company newsletter or during meetings, an associate "wall of fame," paid trips, certificates of achievement, gift certificates, honorary lunches or dinners, letters of recognition, and trophies or plaques. Have fun with the program and make associates feel special by recognizing them for their efforts, whether for effective teamwork, financial results or measures, personal excellence, character (loyalty, integrity and respect), or stewardship (good use of resources, including cash, equipment, safety, and cleanliness). Service awards should be given at a special occasion, such as a reception to which the entire company is invited. Reflect on the company's successes and honor all the great employees who have made it possible. Publicly recognize associates who are celebrating milestones at SYSCO (5, 10, 15, 20, 25 years of service). Consider the following when structuring a recognition program:

- *Associate eligibility:* Do all participating associates have an equal chance of "winning"?

- *Award criteria:* What behavior(s) do you want to recognize and reinforce? Rewarded behaviors should be consistent with SYSCO's values and culture.

- *Nomination and review process:* What will be the selection process for winners?

- *Number of recipients:* How many associates will be eligible for recognitions or rewards?

- *Actual awards:* Are the rewards truly rewarding? Some operating companies ask their associates when hired what is motivating to them.

- *Program management and budget:* Are the rewards given in a timely manner? How much does the company want to spend on the program(s)?

- *Communication:* Is there clear communication about the program details? Does the program publicly recognize associates? If so, make sure the event is highly publicized.

- *Success:* Measure and evaluate whether recognition or reward program was successful.

- *ABC Program for Warehouse:* Implement activity-based compensation (ABC) for warehouse employees. By offering additional incentives, you can reward appropriate behaviors. *(Web site: ABC PowerPoint Slide Presentation)*

- *Internal Job Postings/SYSCO S.T.E.P.:* Evaluate the current internal job posting system and clearly identify positions that will be posted internally. Note that all positions below the director level should be posted. Be consistent in your posting practices. Communicate with and train the appropriate managers as to their responsibilities with the posting system. Posting jobs on a consistent basis improves employee morale and perceptions of the selection/promotion process. For those who self-select to utilize SYSCO S.T.E.P., ensure that you support their interest in the program and in being a front-line supervisor. *(Web site: Front-Line Supervisor Development Program SYSCO S.T.E.P. Operations Workbook)*

5-STAR Actions to Impact Inclusion through Engagement and Diversity

Orientation Program (See description above.)

*Employee Advocate Meetings (Non-Union Companies Only): Conduct meetings with key associates who can give early warning signs if third-party intervention problems appear to be likely. *(Web site: Diversity and Industry Relations Report)*

SYSCO S.T.E.P. Program (See description above.)

Employee Feedback Programs (See description above.)

5-STAR Actions to Impact Inclusion through Engagement and Diversity, continued

Recruitment Strategy: Develop a company recruitment strategy and identify different types of recruiting sources that would work best for your company. For example, involve associates in the hiring process by establishing a referral program in which employees receive a bonus when someone they refer is hired, and then a larger bonus after the new person has completed several months on the job. Employees are more likely to remain with and feel committed to a company where they are part of the associate selection process.

Targeted Selection: Utilize targeted selection as your operating company's selection process for employees. Targeted selection allows us to better match candidates to the job criteria or competencies through the use of carefully designed interview guides, motivational profile assessments, and careful analysis of candidate data. Through the proper selection of employees, we can ensure a stronger and more committed workforce.

Community Involvement: Contribute to the local community by participating in local events and charities. Employees appreciate companies that invest in the community, and such behaviors benefit the workplace and the community. Organize a blood drive and accommodate employees' work schedules so they can donate blood. Participate in events that will promote the company as a great employer and reinforce outside individuals' opinion that the company is a great place to have a career.

*Business Case for Diversity: Reinforce leadership's commitment to diversity by driving diversity awareness throughout your organization. To achieve double-digit sales growth, respond to industry growth, build and leverage the changing demographic base, and remain proactive on liability issues, we must continue to leverage and expand our diversity. This includes a business strategy focusing on improving the diversity of our leadership, our community, our suppliers, and our workforce. One very effective way to reinforce the commitment to diversity is to consistently communicate and demonstrate support for the business case for diversity. Include the diversity business case, a presentation explaining the importance of diversity, as a staff meeting agenda item. Model the behaviors consistent with being a leader who values diversity and coach and provide feedback to those whose behavior is not consistent with respect for diversity. *(Web site: Diversity and Industry Relations Report)*

Resources

Beatty, Richard W., Brian E. Becker, and Mark A. Huselid. 2005. *Workforce Scorecard: Managing Human Capital to Execute Strategy.* Cambridge, MA: Harvard Business School Press.

Collins, Jim. 2001. *Good to Great: Why Some Companies Make the Leap…and Others Don't.* New York: HarperCollins.

Essentials of Finance and Budgeting: Business Literacy for HR Professionals. 2005. Alexandria, VA: Society for Human Resource Management and Cambridge, MA: Harvard Business School Press.

Essentials of Managing Change and Transition: Business Literacy for HR Professionals. 2005. Alexandria, VA: Society for Human Resource Management and Cambridge, MA: Harvard Business School Press.

Essentials of Negotiation: Business Literacy for HR Professionals. 2005. Alexandria, VA: Society for Human Resource Management and Cambridge, MA: Harvard Business School Press.

Fitz-enz, Jac. 1990. *Human Value Management: The Value-Adding Human Resource Management Strategy for the 1990s.* Hoboken, NJ: Jossey-Bass.

Fitz-enz, Jac. 2000. *The ROI of Human Capital: Measuring the Economic Value of Employee Performance.* New York: AMACOM.

Fleming, Maureen J., and Jennifer B. Wilson. 2001. *Effective HR Measurement Techniques.* Alexandria, VA: Society for Human Resource Management.

Greer, Charles R. 2000. *Strategic Human Resource Management: A General Managerial Perspective.* Upper Saddle River, NJ: Prentice Hall.

Grundy, Tony and Laura Brown. 2003. *Value-Based Human Resource Strategy: Developing Your HR Consultancy Role*. Burlington, MA: Butterworth-Heinemann.

Gubman, Edward L. 1998. *The Talent Solution: Aligning Strategy and People to Achieve Extraordinary Results*. New York: McGraw-Hill Trade.

Heskett, James L., W. Earl Sasser, and Leonard A. Schlesinger. 2002. *The Value Profit Chain: Treat Employees Like Customers and Customers Like Employees*. New York: Simon & Schuster.

Holbeche, Linda. 2001. *Aligning Human Resources and Business Strategy*. Burlington, MA: Butterworth-Heinemann.

Kaplan, Robert S., and David P. Norton. 1996. *Balanced Scorecard: Translating Strategy into Action*. Cambridge, MA: Harvard Business School Press.

Kenton, Barbara, and Jane Yarnall. 2005. *HR— The Business Partner: Shaping a New Direction*. Burlington, MA: Elsevier.

Kravetz, Dennis J. 2004. *Measuring Human Capital: Converting Work Place Behavior into Dollars*. Scottsdale, AZ: Kravetz Associates.

Lawler, Edward E. III. 2003. *Creating a Strategic Human Resources Organization: An Assessment of Trends and New Directions*. Palo Alto, CA: Stanford University Press.

Phillips, Jack J. 2005. *Investing in Your Company's Human Capital: Strategies to Avoid Spending Too Little or Too Much*. New York: AMACOM.

Phillips, Jack J. 2005. *The Human Resources Scorecard: Measuring the Return on Investment*. Burlington, MA: Butterworth-Heinemann.

Phillips, Jack J., and Jac Fitz-enz. 1998. *A New Vision for Human Resources: Defining the Human Resources Function by Its Results*. Boston: Crisp Learning.

Phillips, Jack J., and Patricia Pulliam Phillips. 2005. *Proving the Value of HR: How and Why to Measure ROI*. Alexandria, VA: Society for Human Resource Management.

Robinson, James C., and Dana Gaines Robinson. 2005. *Strategic Business Partner: Aligning People Strategies with Business Goals*. San Francisco: Berrett-Koehler.

Rothwell, William J., and David D. Dubois. 2004. *Competency-Based Human Resource Management*. Mountain View, CA: Davies-Black.

Seagraves, Theresa. 2004. *Quick! Show Me Your Value*. Alexandria, VA: ASTD and the Society for Human Resource Management.

Sullivan, John. 2004. *Rethinking Strategic HR: HR's Role in Building a Performance Culture*. Riverwoods, IL: CCH.

Ulrich, Dave and Wayne Brockbank. 2005. *The HR Value Proposition.* Cambridge, MA: Harvard Business School Press.

Ulrich, Dave, Brian E. Becker, and Mark A. Huselid. 2001. *HR Scorecard: Linking People, Strategy, and Performance.* Cambridge, MA: Harvard Business School Press.

Ulrich, Dave, Michael R. Losey, and Susan R. Meisinger. 2005. *Future of Human Resource Management: 64 Thought Leaders Explore the Critical HR Issues of Today and Tomorrow.* Alexandria, VA: Society for Human Resource Management and Hoboken, NJ: John Wiley & Sons.

Weatherly, Leslie A. 2003. *Research Quarterly—Human Capital—The Elusive Asset: Measuring and Managing Human Capital: A Strategic Imperative for HR.* Alexandria, VA: Society for Human Resource Management.

Weatherly, Leslie A. 2003. *Research Quarterly—The Value of People: The Challenges and Opportunities of Human Capital Measurement and Reporting.* Alexandria, VA: Society for Human Resource Management.

Withers, Mark, Mark Williamson, and Martin Reddington. 2004. *Transforming HR: Creating Value through People.* Burlington, MA: Elsevier.

Yorks, Lyle. 2004. *Strategic Human Resource Development: Building Performance Capability through Strategically Targeted HRD.* Mason, OH: Thomson Learning.

References

Bartlett, C. A., and U. S. Rangan. 1985. "Komatsu Ltd." Harvard Business School Case No. 9-385-277, Cambridge, MA.

Bethune, G. 1998. *From Worst to First: Behind the Scenes of Continental's Remarkable Comeback.* New York: John Wiley & Sons.

Brannigan, M., and E. Lisser. 1996. "Ground Control: Cost Cutting at Delta Raises Stock Price but Lowers the Service." *Wall Street Journal,* June 20, A1.

Brannigan, M., and J. White. 1997. "So Be It: Why Delta Air Lines Decided It Was Time For CEO to Take Off." *Wall Street Journal,* May 30, A1.

Chang, V., and C. O'Reilly. 2001. "Seibel Systems: Culture as a Pillar of Success." Stanford Business School, Case No. HR-14, Stanford, CA.

Collins, J. 2001. *Good to Great: Why Some Companies Make the Leap and Others Don't.* New York: HarperCollins.

The Corporate Leadership Council, Corporate Executive Board. 2002. "Key Findings: Building the High-Performance Workforce: A Quantitative Analysis of the Effectiveness of Performance Management Strategies." www.corporateleadershipcouncil.com.

Delery, J. E., and D. H. Doty. 1996. "Modes of Theorizing in Strategic Human Resource Management: Tests of Universalistic, Contingency and Configurational Performance Predictions." *Academy of Management Journal,* 39:802–35.

Drucker, P. 2003. *The Essential Drucker: The Best of Sixty Years of Peter Drucker's Essential Writings on Management.* New York: HarperBusiness.

Fulmer, B., B. Gerhart, and K. Scott. 2003. "Are the 100 Best Better? An Empirical Investigation of the Relationship between Being a 'Great Place to Work' and Firm Performance." *Personnel Psychology*, 56:965–93.

The Gallup Organization. 2001. "What Your Disaffected Workers Cost." *Gallup Management Journal*, March 15. (Nationally representative sample of 1,000 employed adults, October 2000. Margin of error plus or minus three percentage points.)

Guthrie, J. 2001. "High Involvement Work Practices, Turnover, and Productivity: Evidence from New Zealand." *Academy of Management Journal*, 44:180–92.

Hartline, M. D., B. R. Woolridge, and K. C. Jones. 2003. "Guest Perceptions of Hotel Quality: Determining Which Employee Groups Count Most." *Cornell Hotel and Restaurant Administration Quarterly*, 44: 43–53.

Heskett, J. L., T. O. Jones, G. W. Loveman, W. E. Sasser, Jr., and L. A. Schlesinger. 1994. "Putting the Service-Profit Chain to Work." *Harvard Business Review*, (March–April). 164–74.

Heskett, J. L., W. E. Sasser, Jr., and L.A. Schlesinger. 1997. *The Service Profit Chain: How Leading Companies Link Profit and Growth to Loyalty, Satisfaction, and Value.* New York: Free Press.

Heskett, J .L., Sasser, W. E. Jr., L. A. Schlesinger. 2005. *The Value Profit Chain: Treat Employees Like Customers and Customers Like Employees.* New York: Free Press.

Holmes, S., D. Bennett, K. Carlisle, and C. Dawson. 2002. "Planet Starbucks." *Business Week*, September 9.

Huselid, M. A. 1995. "The Impact of Human Resource Management Practices on Turnover, Productivity, Corporate Financial Performance." *Academy of Management Journal*, 38:635–72.

Kaplan, R. S., and D. P. Norton. 1996. *The Balanced Scorecard: Translating Strategy into Action.* Cambridge, MA: Harvard Business School Press.

MacDuffie, J. P. 1995. "Human Resource Bundles and Manufacturing Performance: Organizational Logic and Flexible Production Systems in the World Auto Industry." *Industrial and Labor Relations Review*, 48:197–221.

Nelson, B. 2005. *1001 Ways to Reward Your Employees*, 2nd edition. New York: Workman Publishing.

O'Reilly, C., and J. Pfeffer. 2000. *Hidden Value: How Great Companies Achieve Extraordinary Results with Ordinary People.* Cambridge, MA: Harvard Business School Press.

Rafaeli, A. 1989. "When Cashiers Meet Customers: An Analysis of the Role of Supermarket Cashiers." *Academy of Management Journal*, 32: 245–73.

Rogg, K. L, D. B. Schmidt, C. Shull, and N. Schmitt. 2001. "Human Resource Practices, Organizational Climate, and Customer Satisfaction." *Journal of Management*, 27: 431–49.

Ryan, A. M., M. J. Schmit, and R. Johnson. 1996. "Attitudes and Effectiveness: Examining Relations at an Organizational Level." *Personnel Psychology*, 49: 853–81.

Schlesinger, L., and J. Zornitsky. 1991. "Job Satisfaction, Service Capability, and Customer Satisfaction: An Examination of Linkages and Management Implications." *Human Resource Planning*, 14: 141–50.

Schmit, M., and S. Allscheid. 1995. "Employee Attitudes and Customer Satisfaction: Making Theoretical and Empirical Connections." *Personnel Psychology*, 48: 521–36.

Schneider, B., and D. Bowen. 1985. "Employee and Customer Perceptions of Service in Banks: Replication and Extension." *Journal of Applied Psychology*, 70: 423–33.

Schneider, B., S. S. White, and M. C. Paul. 1998. "Linking Service Climate and Customer Perceptions of Service Quality: Test of a Causal Model." *Journal of Applied Psychology*, 83: 150–63.

Schultz, H., and D. Yang. 1997. *Pour Your Heart into It: How Starbucks Built a Company One Cup at a Time*. New York: Hyperion.

Starbucks Corporate Social Responsibility Report. 2004. http://www.starbucks.com/aboutus/CSR2004_Sec5Workplace.pdf.

Starbucks Corporation Fiscal 2004 Annual Report. 2005. http://www.starbucks.com/aboutus/investor.asp.

Ulrich, D. 1997. *Human Resource Champions*. Cambridge, MA: Harvard Business School Press.

Verespej, M. 1994. "How the Best Got Better." *Industry Week*, 243 (5): 27–28.

Watson Wyatt. 2001. "Watson Wyatt Human Capital Index®: Human Capital as a Lead Indicator of Shareholder Value." http://www.watsonwyatt.com/research/resrender.asp?id=W-488&page=3.

Wright, P., G. McMahan, S. Snell, and B. Gerhart. 1997. "Strategic Human Resource Management: Building Human Capital and Organizational Capability." Technical report, Cornell University. Ithaca, NY.

Index

About the Authors

Ken Carrig is an executive vice president and chief administrative officer of SYSCO Corporation, a thirty billion dollar food service marketing and distribution organization. He holds a B.S. degree in Labor Economics from Cornell University School of Industrial and Labor Relations. Ken was recently installed in the 2004 Class of Fellows by the National Academy of Human Resources in recognition of his sustained contributions to the broad field of human resources. He is a member of the advisory boards of the University of South Carolina's MBA School, Cornell University's School of Industrial and Labor Relations, the University of Southern California's Center of Organizational Effectiveness, and the Human Resource Policy Association.

Ken's article "HR for the 21st Century" was published in *HR Magazine*. He also worked with Wayne Cascio of the University of Colorado and the SHRM Foundation to create an educational DVD entitled "HR in Alignment...The Link to Business Results" that has been used by universities and executive programs around the world.

Prior to joining SYSCO Corporation, Ken was part of the turnaround team that was recruited by Continental Airlines; he was global vice president of human resources at Continental from January 1995 to September 1997. In 1997, Continental Airlines' human resources department received the Service Optimas Award for being a premier service provider and making significant contributions to Continental's successful turnaround from "the worst to first" airline in the industry. Ken was employed with PepsiCo for approximately ten years, including five years with Frito-Lay, three years at PepsiCo world headquarters, and two years with Taco Bell.

Patrick M. Wright is Professor of Human Resource Studies and Director of the Center for Advanced Human Resource Studies in the School of Industrial and Labor Relations, Cornell University. He holds a B.A. in psychology from Wheaton College, and an MBA and a Ph.D. in Organizational Behavior/Human Resource Management from Michigan State University.

Patrick teaches, conducts research, and consults in the area of strategic human resource management, focusing on how firms use people as a source of competitive advantage. He has published over 50 research articles in journals such as *Academy of Management Journal, Academy of Management Review, Strategic Management Journal, Organizational Behavior and Human Decision Processes, Journal of Applied Psychology, Personnel Psychology,* and *Journal of Management.* He has contributed over 20 chapters in books and edited volumes. Patrick also has co-authored two textbooks and has co-edited a number of special issues of journals dealing with the future of strategic human resources management and corporate social responsibility. He currently serves on the editorial boards of eight journals.

He has taught in executive development programs at Cornell University, University of Southern California, and Texas A&M and has conducted programs or consulted for several large public and private sector organizations. In addition, he has served as the Chair of the HR Division of the Academy of Management and on the boards of directors for the SHRM Foundation, World at Work, and the Human Resource Planning Society.

Additional 5-STAR Materials

To see additional, detailed materials that support SYSCO's 5-STAR Company efforts, go to the SHRM Web site at www.shrm.org/books/buildingprofit/tools.

Selected Additional Titles from the Society for Human Resource Management (SHRM®)

Diverse Teams at Work
By Lee Gardenswartz and Anita Rowe

The Future of Human Resources Management
Editors David Ulrich, Mike Losey, and Sue Meisinger

HR Source Book Series
Performance Appraisal Source Book
By Mike Deblieux
HIPAA Privacy Source Book
By William S. Hubbartt, SPHR, CCP
Hiring Source Book
By Cathy Fyock, CAP, SPHR
Trainer's Diversity Source Book
By Jonamay Lambert, M.A. and Selma Myers, M.A.

Harvard/SHRM Series on Business Literacy for HR Professionals
Series Advisor Wendy Bliss, J.D., SPHR
Essentials of Finance and Budgeting
Essentials of Managing Change and Transition
Essentials of Negotiation

Human Resource Essentials: Your Guide to Starting and Running the HR Function
By Lin Grensing-Pophal, SPHR

Manager of Choice: 5 Competencies for Cultivating Top Talent
By Nancy S. Ahlrichs

Managing Employee Retention: A Strategic Accountability Approach
By Jack J. Phillips, Ph.D. and Adele O. Connell, Ph.D.

Practical HR Series
Legal, Effective References: How to Give and Get Them
By Wendy Bliss, J.D., SPHR
Investigating Workplace Harassment: How to Be Fair, Thorough, and Legal
By Amy Oppenheimer, J.D., and Craig Pratt, MSW, SPHR
Proving the Value of HR: How and Why to Measure ROI
By Jack J. Phillips, Ph.D. and Patricia Pulliam Phillips, Ph.D.

Responsible Restructuring: Creative and Profitable Alternatives to Layoffs
By Wayne F. Cascio

Retaining Your Best Employees (In Action Case Studies)
Series Editor Jack J. Phillips

Supervisor's Guide to Labor Relations
By T.O. Collier, Jr.

Understanding the Federal Wage & Hour Laws: What Employers Must Know about FLSA and its Overtime Regulations
By Seyfarth Shaw LLP

To Order SHRM Books

SHRM offers a member discount on all books that it publishes or sells. To order this or any other book published by the Society, contact the SHRMStore.®

Online: www.shrm.org/shrmstore
By Phone: 800-444-5006 (option #1); or 770-442-8633 (ext. 362);
              or TDD 703-548-6999
By Fax: 770-442-9742
By Mail: SHRM Distribution Center
              P.O. Box 930132
              Atlanta, GA 31193-0132
              USA